D1499367

THE REVOLUTIONARY WAR AND GEORGE WASHINGTON'S ARMY IN AMERICAN HISTORY

The IN AMERICAN HISTORY Series

IN
AMERICAN
HISTORY

THE REVOLUTIONARY WAR AND GEORGE WASHINGTON'S ARMY IN AMERICAN HISTORY

Tom McGowen

Enslow Publishers, Inc.

40 Industrial Road   PO Box 38
Box 398   Aldershot
Berkeley Heights, NJ 07922   Hants GU12 6BP
USA   UK

http://www.enslow.com

DEER PARK PUBLIC LIBRARY
44 LAKE AVENUE
DEER PARK, N.Y. 11729

Copyright © 2004 by Tom McGowen

All rights reserved.

No part of this book may be reproduced by any means
without the written permission of the publisher.

Library of Congress Cataloging-in-Publication Data

McGowen, Tom.
    The Revolutionary War and George Washington's Army in American
history/ Tom McGowen.
        p. cm.—(In American history)
    Summary: Details the pivotal role that George Washington played
during the American Revolution and the consequences of his involvement.
    Includes bibliographical references and index.
    ISBN 0-7660-2143-2
    1. United States—History—Revolution, 1775–1783—Campaigns—
Juvenile literature. 2. United States. Continental Army—History—
Juvenile literature. [1. Washington, George, 1732-1799. 2. United
States—History—Revolution, 1775–1783. 3. United States. Continental
Army.] I. Title. II. Series.
E230.M39   2003
973.3'092—dc21
                                  2003007221

Printed in the United States of America

10 9 8 7 6 5 4 3 2 1

To Our Readers: We have done our best to make sure all Internet Addresses in
this book were active and appropriate when we went to press. However, the
author and the publisher have no control over and assume no liability for the
material available on those Internet sites or on other Web sites they may link to.
Any comments or suggestions can be sent by e-mail to comments@enslow.com or
to the address on the back cover.

Illustration Credits: Enslow Publishers, Inc., pp. 6, 21, 55; John
Grafton, *The American Revolution: A Picture Sourcebook,* New York:
Dover Publications, Inc., 1975, pp. 11, 30, 36, 44, 53, 57, 84, 96, 108;
National Archives and Records Administration, pp. 9, 16, 19, 47, 67, 73,
75, 88, 90, 91, 109.

Cover Illustration: National Archives and Records Administration
(Large vertical and both horizontal photos); Painting by John Trumball,
courtesy Henry Francis du Pont Winterthur Museum, reproduced from
the *Dictionary of American Portraits,* published by Dover Publications,
Inc., in 1967 (Small vertical photo).

★ CONTENTS ★

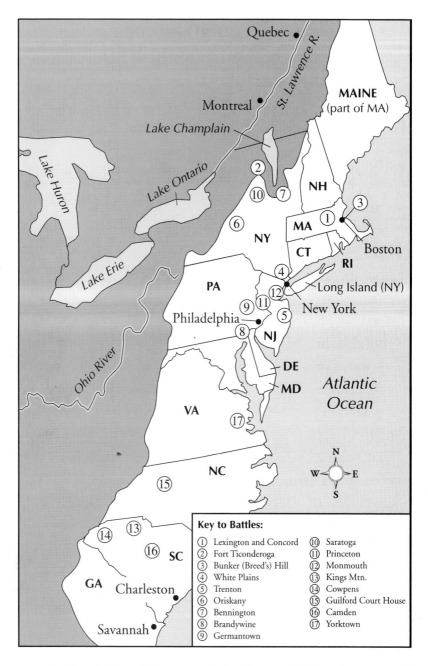

During the Revolutionary War, battles raged throughout the
Thirteen Colonies.

Key to Battles:
① Lexington and Concord
② Fort Ticonderoga
③ Bunker (Breed's) Hill
④ White Plains
⑤ Trenton
⑥ Oriskany
⑦ Bennington
⑧ Brandywine
⑨ Germantown
⑩ Saratoga
⑪ Princeton
⑫ Monmouth
⑬ Kings Mtn.
⑭ Cowpens
⑮ Guilford Court House
⑯ Camden
⑰ Yorktown

AN APRIL MORNING IN 1775

In the early morning darkness on April 19, 1775, a man lay sleeping in a large house on high ground overlooking a river. He was a big man, standing six feet two inches tall and weighing over two hundred pounds. He was forty-three years old. Large areas of farmland surrounded his house, and he was a prosperous farmer, growing tobacco and several kinds of fruit. His name was George Washington.

Washington lived in America, in what was known as the colony of Virginia. A colony is an area of land that belongs to another nation. Virginia belonged to the nation of Great Britain, which consisted of the countries of the British Isles—England, Scotland, Ireland, and Wales. Virginia was one of the British colonies that stretched along the coast of North America. They were the homes of many people who had come from the British Isles and other places. The colonies were ruled by the British government. Each colony had a governor, who was responsible to the British king, George III, and some British troops stationed there, to keep order. There was no American army, no American president or Congress. Most Americans thought of themselves as British citizens, subjects of King George.

Besides being a farmer, George Washington was an elected member of his colony's government. For fifteen years, he had served as a representative of the people of his district in Virginia, helping make laws and solve problems. He had also served in the Virginia militia.

The militia was a system that provided for the defense of a colony. It had begun in the early days of the colonies, when there was often danger of American Indian raids on colonial villages. Every able-bodied male from sixteen to sixty was considered a member of the militia, or a militiaman. Every militiaman was expected to become a soldier in the event of danger, and to have his own musket, powder, and bullets. Militiamen did not have uniforms. Most regions had a militia company, men who got together once a year to practice shooting and marching. But for the most part the training was very poor, and the meetings generally turned into picnics!

Colonel Washington

Washington was an officer of the militia when what was known as the French and Indian War began in America in 1754. British troops and American militia fought together against French forces aided by several American Indian tribes. Washington was in combat in several battles, and eventually was appointed colonel

George Washington

in command of the entire Virginia militia. He took charge of defending Virginia against attacks by France's American Indian allies. However, he never had more than several hundred men, because many militiamen would not show up for duty when called. When the war and the danger ended, Washington resigned as a militia officer. But he had become America's most famous soldier.

Thus, George Washington was a well-known and respected man in Virginia. He was happily married, and his life was pleasant and secure. But as Washington lay sleeping on the morning of April 19, something that was going to change his life was taking place some five hundred miles away. It would also change the lives of most people in America.

The Minutemen of Massachusetts

A man and a teenage boy stood on a grassy field in a little village called Lexington, in the colony of Massachusetts. The boy began banging out a rattling beat on a military drum. Shortly, figures came trotting through the darkness from all parts of the village. Before long, seventy men stood in two ragged lines stretching across the grassy field. Except for the young drummer, every man was armed with a long gun, known as a musket.

The men were militiamen, but they were special. They trained and practiced being soldiers several times a week instead of once a year. They called themselves "minutemen"—men who had agreed to fight an

American militiamen were mainly farmers and workingmen who got together from time to time to learn to be soldiers. They had no uniforms, but most of them knew how to handle a musket.

enemy at a minute's notice. Like most militiamen, they had no uniforms, but were all simply wearing their everyday clothes. Most had on what were known as tricorns—three-cornered hats—with broad brims that were turned up and squeezed together, forming a point at each side and one in front. Their shirts were of white linen with wide sleeves that most men had rolled up to their elbows. Their tight-fitting pants, called breeches, reached only to the knee and were made of coarse black, brown, or gray cloth. Heavy wool stockings of white or gray covered their lower legs. On their feet were square-toed shoes of ox-hide dyed black or brown.

The Redcoats of King George III

The enemy the minutemen anticipated was no more than half a mile away and coming straight toward them. It was a long column of seven hundred men, tramping down a dirt road that ran through a forest.[1] They wore uniforms consisting of long-tailed orange-red coats, white breeches, and white stockings protected by black, calf-high, buttoned leggings. This was the uniform of the British Army, generally regarded as the best army in the world. Because of the color of their coats, the British soldiers earned the nickname of "redcoats" throughout the colonies.

Only a dozen years earlier, British soldiers could have marched along any road in Massachusetts in broad daylight and met with a friendly atmosphere. But now they were moving through darkness so they would not be seen. Things were not going well between the American colonies and the British government that these soldiers represented. The colonists had refused to pay certain taxes and do other things required by the government of King George III. This had resulted in harsh measures against the colonies of Massachusetts and New York, and all the other colonies felt threatened. Many colonists belonged to the political group known as Whigs, which opposed the British form of government. (Their opponents, loyal to the British government, were called Tories, or loyalists.) Some Whigs were even beginning to talk about breaking entirely free from British rule and governing themselves.

Of course, this would quite simply mean war, for the king would never allow his colonies to break free from his rule. He himself had once said it would take "blows"—armed combat—to keep the colonies tied to Britain.[2] But many colonists were ready to fight for freedom if necessary. Many militia companies throughout the northern colonies had stored up ammunition in case they ever did have to fight.

The column of British soldiers marching along had been sent out to seize such a store of ammunition that a spy had reported was hidden in the town of Concord. To reach Concord, the soldiers would have to pass through Lexington.

A Face-Off in Lexington

The soldiers entered Lexington just as dawn was flooding the sky with light. They soon reached the park-like, grassy field known as the Green, where two lines of seventy armed minutemen were standing alongside the road to Concord.

The Americans had been warned that the British were coming by the efforts of two colonists, Paul Revere and William Dawes. These men had risked capture, imprisonment, and even death to ride on horseback through the night to alert the minutemen of every nearby village that the soldiers were on the way.

At the head of the British column rode Major John Pitcairn of the British marines. Spurring his horse forward, he shouted a command. The soldiers immediately spread out to form a line of three rows, one behind another, facing the Americans. This was the battle formation for troops of a European army. To attack, troops in this formation marched straight toward the enemy, with a band playing a military march to help the men keep in perfect step. When men were shot and fell to the ground, the others moved around them or stepped over them and kept right on going. When they were close enough, the officer leading the attack shouted a command. Every soldier lowered his musket so that its bayonet, the long, sharp, swordlike blade attached to the musket's muzzle, pointed straight at the enemy. With a loud yell of "hurrah!" from hundreds of voices, the attacking troops would begin to move at a slow run. The sight of those gleaming bayonets suddenly coming at them was often enough to make the enemy simply run away in panic!

"Lay down your arms!" Pitcairn yelled at the Americans.[3] The British were outraged that they were apparently trying to keep the king's troops from proceeding to Concord to do what they had been sent to do. The muskets of Pitcairn's men were loaded and cocked, and so were those of the minutemen. It is said that their commander, John Parker, told them, "Don't fire unless fired upon. But if they want to have a war, let it begin here!"[4] However, this may not be true.

The Weapon of the Eighteenth Century

The main weapon used by the British and the Americans was what is known as a smoothbore musket. It was about three feet, eight inches long and fired a one-ounce lead ball. After firing, it had to be reloaded each time. This was rather complicated. First, the flintlock, a hammerlike device with a piece of flint-stone in it, had to be half cocked, by pulling it back. Next, a cartridge was pulled from a container hanging at the soldier's right hip. The cartridge was a paper cylinder with a quantity of gunpowder and a ball inside it. The soldier tore the cartridge open with his teeth. He sprinkled a tiny amount of gunpowder into a small opening on the musket barrel in front of the flintlock. Then, he pulled a long iron rod, called a ram-rod, out of a socket under the barrel. He used it to push the powder, ball, and wadded-up cartridge all the way down to the end of the barrel. Finally, he shoved the ramrod back into its socket and fully cocked the flintlock. When he pulled the trigger, the flintlock snapped forward, striking the steel edge of the small opening the powder had been sprinkled on. This caused sparks that ignited the powder in the barrel, causing an explosion that drove the ball out. A trained soldier could load and shoot about three times a minute.

In a battle, a British unit of several hundred men, called a regiment, all fired at the same time on an offi-cer's command. This was called a volley. It sent hundreds of bullets slamming into a formation of enemy soldiers. Volleys were generally fired at a dis-tance of no more than thirty or forty yards, and could cause a large number of casualties—dead and wounded soldiers.

A Shot That Started a War

For a few moments as the Americans and British soldiers faced each other, nothing happened. Then, without any command being given, there was a shot. It is not known whether it was a British soldier or minuteman who fired. But immediately, the British soldiers fired a volley. There was a sputter of return shots from the minutemen. Then they scattered off into the village, realizing that they could not stand against hundreds of soldiers. Cursing and beating men with the flat of his sword, Pitcairn ordered them to stop firing. He was enraged that they had fired without

The Revolutionary War began when a British force encountered seventy Massachusetts minutemen blocking the road through the village of Lexington.

an order and had killed many Americans. Eight minutemen were dead and ten others were wounded; one British soldier had a slight wound.

After a time, the British continued their march to Concord, arriving about eight o'clock in the morning. A number of soldiers were sent to search every house for the hidden ammunition supply. They did not find it; it had been buried in a field. However, they did

SOURCE DOCUMENT

I, JOHN ROBINS, BEING OF LAWFUL AGE, DO TESTIFYE [SIC], [THAT] THERE SUDDENLY APPEAR'D A NUMBER OF THE KINGS TROOPS, ABOUT A THOUSAND, AS I THOUGHT, AT THE DISTANCE OF ABOUT 60 OR 70 YARDS FROM US HUZZAING [SHOUTING], AND ON A QUICK PACE TOWARDS US, WITH THREE OFFICERS IN THEIR FRONT ON HORSE BACK, AND ON FULL GALLOP TOWARDS US, THE FOREMOST OF WHICH CRYED [SIC], THROW DOWN YOUR ARMS YE VILLAINS, YE REBELS! UPON WHICH SAID COMPANY DISPERSING, THE FOREMOST OF THE THREE OFFICERS ORDER'D THEIR MEN, SAYING, FIRE, BY GOD, FIRE! AT WHICH MOMENT WE RECEIVED A VERY HEAVY AND CLOSE FIRE FROM THEM, AT WHICH INSTANT, BEING WOUNDED, I FELL, AND SEVERAL OF OUR MEN WERE SHOT DEAD BY ME. CAPTAIN PARKER'S MEN I BELIEVE HAD NOT THEN FIRED A GUN, . . .[5]

In a statement dated April 25, 1775, minuteman John Robins describes his frontline experience at the short battle of Lexington. It was submitted to the Second Continental Congress and read aloud on Thursday, May 11, 1775, along with a number of other militiamen's statements.

find some gun carriages—wooden wheeled supports for cannons—which they chopped up and set on fire.

By now, groups of militia and minutemen from nearby towns had begun to collect in the hills around Concord. They saw the smoke of the fires and believed the British were burning the town. There were yells of rage. "Are you going to let them burn the town down?" a man demanded.[6]

The Americans came streaming down out of the hills. Before long, the crack of musket shots was shattering the air. At the bridge outside the town, two minutemen and three soldiers were killed and ten soldiers wounded. The British got into formation and began to march back toward Lexington. Minutemen by the hundreds trailed behind them and stalked alongside them at a distance.

The British Army Meets a New Kind of Warfare

The march from Concord back to Lexington turned into a nightmare for the British. They had expected the Americans to come marching at them as a European army would. But the Americans had fired at the column of soldiers from behind houses, trees, and walls. The road behind the marching column became littered with the motionless bodies of dead redcoats. Most British were not used to this kind of warfare, which Americans had learned from fighting American Indians. The only thing the British officers could do was send groups of soldiers out on each side of the column to try to drive the minutemen off. A few Americans were caught and stabbed with bayonets, but most simply trotted away for a time, then came back and resumed firing. The number of dead and wounded British soldiers continued to grow.

The number of attacking minutemen also continued to grow, as more and more armed colonists came flocking to the sound of banging muskets. Even as the fighting was going on at Concord, colonials on fast horses were galloping up back roads in all directions. They yelled out news of the battle and urged every man they saw to come at once. Many farmers out

After the Battle at Concord Bridge, the British marched out of the city. The minutemen followed them, firing from behind trees and houses on both sides of the road.

plowing their fields ran to get their muskets and ammunition, and took off at a jog. Militia companies assembled on village greens and marched off. Men with horses saddled up and set off at a gallop.

Luckily for the British, help had been sent. Nearly fourteen hundred British troops, with several cannons, were waiting at Lexington. A cannon was a very large gun on a wooden, wheeled platform. It could shoot a large, iron ball a distance of about nine hundred yards. A ball could smash through four or five men at a time in a formation of soldiers, killing and mangling them. Cannons could also fire balls that exploded, as well as dozens of small lead balls at a time. A cannon was loaded much as a musket was, with powder rammed into the barrel and a ball pushed down on top of it. To fire, the tip of a burning piece of rope was pushed into a hole in the top of the barrel, igniting the powder inside. A cannon could only be fired about twice a minute, but the presence of cannons was fearsome to the minutemen.

An American Victory

If there had been a minuteman commander to tell the Americans what to do, they might have been able to organize an attack that could actually have destroyed the entire British force. However, the minutemen were all acting in small groups and had no idea of their strength. The British force seemed too much for them, and they held back. The British soldiers who had been at Concord took refuge behind their rescuers and flung

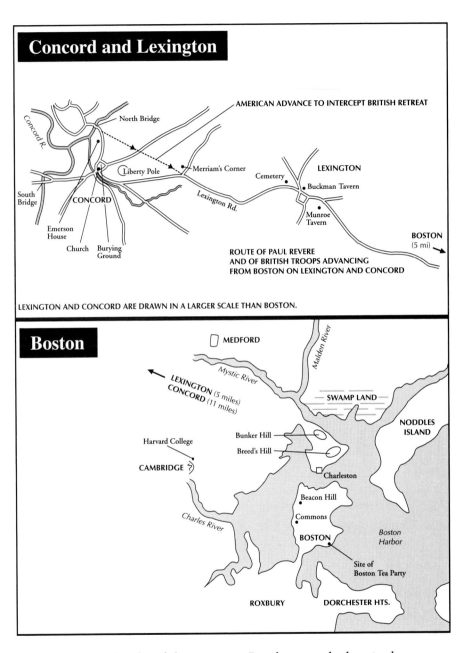

Concord and Lexington

AMERICAN ADVANCE TO INTERCEPT BRITISH RETREAT

Concord R.

North Bridge

Liberty Pole

Merriam's Corner

Cemetery

LEXINGTON

Buckman Tavern

South Bridge

CONCORD

Lexington Rd.

Munroe Tavern

Emerson House

BOSTON (5 mi)

Church   Burying Ground

ROUTE OF PAUL REVERE
AND OF BRITISH TROOPS ADVANCING
FROM BOSTON ON LEXINGTON AND CONCORD

LEXINGTON AND CONCORD ARE DRAWN IN A LARGER SCALE THAN BOSTON.

Boston

MEDFORD

Malden River

Mystic River

LEXINGTON (5 miles)
CONCORD (11 miles)

SWAMP LAND

NODDLES ISLAND

Bunker Hill

Breed's Hill

Harvard College

CAMBRIDGE

Charleston

Beacon Hill

Commons

Charles River

Boston Harbor

BOSTON

Site of
Boston Tea Party

ROXBURY   DORCHESTER HTS.

The first battles of the American Revolution took place in the Boston area.

themselves on the ground, panting like thirsty dogs. After a time, the entire British force began a slow retreat back to the city of Boston. The Americans followed them, continuing to fire from behind trees and fences, killing and wounding as many soldiers as they could.

The British soldiers finally reached safety, but a total of 273 men had been killed, were wounded, or were missing.[7] The minutemen had a total of ninety-three casualties.[8] It was clearly a victory for the colonists.

Nine days later, George Washington read about the battles of Lexington and Concord in a Virginia newspaper. He felt that after all this bloodshed there was no way an all-out war with Great Britain could be avoided. During the French and Indian War, he had fought alongside British soldiers and had made many British friends. But he was now solidly with the colonists.

BOSTON BESIEGED

Following the events at Lexington Green and Concord, minutemen and militiamen were soon pouring into the Boston area. Men came from towns throughout Massachusetts, as well as the neighboring colonies of New Hampshire, Connecticut, and Rhode Island. Within a week, there were some fifteen thousand men outside the city. The British force of about five thousand was bottled up inside.[1]

In 1775, Boston was a community of around sixteen thousand people, just a small town by today's standards. It occupied a tiny bit of land sticking out into Boston Harbor, connected to the mainland only by a narrow strip known as the Boston Neck. Thus, the city was on a peninsula, almost entirely surrounded by water. Across that water, on the mainland, the American army was encamped around the peninsula in a nine-mile semicircle enclosing Boston on three sides. Boston was besieged—surrounded by an army that had it cut off from the land around it.

The Whig citizens of Massachusetts, like those of most other colonies, had organized what was called a

Provincial Congress for their colony. This was the group of men who would become the government of Massachusetts if the colony ever broke free from Britain. One of the things the congress had already done was select a man to take command of any army that might be formed in Massachusetts. He was Artemas Ward, a judge. Ward was in bed, suffering from the agonizing pain of a kidney stone when he got word of the fighting at Lexington and Concord, and of the army gathering at Boston. Despite his pain, he got up, dressed, and mounted his horse. He rode all night to reach the army and take command of it.

An Army in Need of Organization— and a Plan

Although he was called a general, Ward did not have much real experience in warfare. However, there were other men with the army at Boston who did. Israel Putnam of Connecticut had fought in a dozen campaigns during the French and Indian War. He held the rank of major general in the force that Connecticut had put together. William Prescott and Richard Gridley, both of Massachusetts, had also fought in the war. They were appointed colonels. These men, and others who knew something about being soldiers, now commanded various parts of the American force surrounding Boston.

People were calling the force the "New England Army" or the "Boston Army." But it really was not much of an army. It was basically just a mob of many groups of militiamen from several different colonies. Real armies, such as the British Army, were formed of regiments of several hundred men, divided into a number of smaller units called companies. The colonies had also organized their militia into regiments, but the regiments were all different sizes. Connecticut regiments had a thousand men in ten companies. Rhode Island regiments had only three hundred fifty men in seven or eight companies. New Hampshire regiments were all different from each other.

Even though the American army vastly outnumbered the British, its commanders knew better than to simply send their men charging into Boston. The way into Boston, the Boston Neck, had been well fortified by the British. Eight British warships lay at anchor in Boston Harbor, bristling with cannons. They could pound the shore with deadly fire if troops tried to attack the fortifications. An attack would have been suicide. So, the American army sat around its campfires day after day, its leaders just waiting to see what the British would do.

A British Fort is Captured, Three Generals Arrive in Boston

One of the men who had come into Massachusetts from another colony, a Connecticut militia captain named Benedict Arnold, soon grew bored of just waiting. He started looking for ways to cause trouble for the British. Many of the leaders of Massachusetts and other New England colonies were worried about the possibility of an invasion by a British army from Canada, and Arnold had an idea for preventing this. In the New York colony was a stone fort known as Fort Ticonderoga, which stood in the path of any army coming into New York. It was staffed by a small force of British soldiers, who would let a British army pass. But if it were filled with American troops, it could block an invasion. Arnold talked the Massachusetts leaders into letting him try to capture it for the American cause.

On May 10, a force of eighty-three Connecticut colony men, led by Arnold and another man from Connecticut named Ethan Allen, made a dawn attack on the fort. They caught the British garrison completely by surprise and captured Fort Ticonderoga without firing a shot. Congress appointed Arnold commander of the small force of American soldiers put into the fort.

Meanwhile, at Boston, the waiting came to an end. Five days after the events at Lexington and Concord, the British governor of Massachusetts colony, General Thomas Gage, had sent a report to England by ship. In answer, three troop transport ships arrived from England and dropped anchor in Boston Harbor on the morning of May 25, 1775. They brought twenty-five hundred soldiers and three of Britain's best generals: Major General Sir William Howe, Major General Sir Henry Clinton, and Major General John Burgoyne, known as "Gentleman Johnny." Burgoyne was annoyed that five thousand British troops were being

SOURCE DOCUMENT

. . . WHEREAS SEVERAL INHABITANTS OF THE NORTHERN COLONIES, RESIDING IN THE VICINITY OF TICONDEROGO [TICONDEROGA], . . . IMPELLED BY A JUST REGARD FOR THE DEFENCE [SIC] AND PRESERVATION OF THEMSELVES AND THEIR COUNTRYMEN FROM SUCH IMMINENT DANGERS AND CALAMITIES HAVE TAKEN POSSESSION OF THAT POST, IN WHICH WAS LODGED A QUANTITY OF CANNON AND MILITARY STORES, THAT WOULD HAVE CERTAINLY BEEN USED IN THE INTENDED INVASION OF THESE COLONIES, THIS CONGRESS EARNESTLY RECOMMEND . . . IMMEDIATELY TO CAUSE THE SAID CANNON AND MILITARY STORES TO BE REMOVED FROM TICONDEROGO TO THE SOUTH END . . . OF LAKE GEORGE; AND IF NECESSARY TO APPLY TO THE COLONIES OF NEW HAMPSHIRE, MASSACHUSETTS BAY, AND CONNECTICUT, FOR SUCH AN ADDITIONAL BODY OF FORCES AS WILL BE SUFFICIENT TO ESTABLISH A STRONG POST AT THAT PLACE . . . [2]

On Thursday, May 18, 1775, the Continental Congress acknowledged the taking of Fort Ticonderoga and made recommendations for securing the fort and its military supplies.

cooped up in Boston by ten thousand "peasants," as he called the Americans. "Let us in, we'll soon have elbow room!" he boasted. [3]

The British Hatch a Plan

By this time, things were becoming difficult in Boston. The purpose of the American siege was to keep food or supplies of any kind from getting into the city, so that it would eventually have to surrender. Even though General Gage had allowed many people to leave the city, mostly Whigs, there was not enough food left for those remaining. So, the three newly arrived British generals began to work out a plan for launching an attack to drive off the American army and open up the city to the outside world again.

They finally agreed on General Howe's plan to land two forces on the mainland by boat, one at each end of the American line. The two forces would slowly move toward each other, eliminating all the American troops in their path. This operation was to take place on the morning of Sunday, June 18.

The British did not take any pains to keep this plan secret. A man in Boston who supported the American cause learned of it. Shortly, the information reached General Ward. Two nights before the British attack was to be made, Ward did something that he thought might spoil the British plan.

At a point on the mainland directly across from Boston, a little piece of land shaped somewhat like a pear stuck out into the water. It was known as Charlestown peninsula, because the tiny town of Charlestown was located at one edge of it. Beyond Charlestown were three hills, and just about every part of Boston and Boston Harbor could easily be seen from the two highest hills. It was obvious that cannons placed there would be able to fire down on British troops trying to get into their boats on the day of the attack. This would cause so many casualties the attack would have to be called off. General Ward intended to put cannons on the hill called Bunker Hill. He picked three regiments to go to the hill and build earthworks, thick walls of dirt reinforced with rocks and logs. The earthworks would provide protection for the cannons as they fired at the enemy.

An Unpleasant Surprise for the British

The three regiments were commanded by Colonel Prescott, but he was accompanied by General Putnam and Colonel Gridley. They arrived at the hills a little before midnight, and immediately found a small problem. No one was sure just which hill was Bunker Hill. From men who lived in the area, it was learned that the two bigger hills were both sometimes known as Bunker Hill. Prescott felt sure the real Bunker Hill was the one that was tallest and farthest back, but the range would be too far for cannons placed on that hill. The three officers agreed to fortify the middle hill and put the cannons there. Prescott ordered his men to begin digging on the middle hill, which was actually Breed's Hill (as it is known to this day). They set to work piling up dirt into thick, sloping six-foot high walls, reinforced with logs, with a deep ditch in front of them for added protection.

The night slid slowly by, and the sky grew light enough for things to be seen. A marine standing watch on the British warship HMS *Lively*, in Boston Harbor, stared in momentary shock at the sight that met his eyes. Shortly, *Lively*'s captain was also on deck, peering in disbelief at what was now squatting on the hill that

American soldiers worked through the night of June 16, 1775, to erect a fort at the top of Breed's Hill. This fort put British troops at the mercy of American cannons.

rose over the harbor—a very well constructed and grimly menacing fort.

At once, the captain ordered his men to open fire on the fort, hoping to smash it down. The boom of ten cannons all firing at the same moment woke everyone in Boston. This included Admiral Samuel Graves, commander of the small fleet in the harbor. *Lively* was firing without permission, and Graves grumpily sent word for it to stop. However, some time later, when he got his first look at the fort, he instantly ordered all the ships in the fleet to open fire on it. To his concern, he saw that cannonballs simply bounced off the fort's thick, log-filled walls.

The British Make a New Plan

The fort was nearly complete by now. It was roughly star-shaped, with V-shaped sections of walls sticking out on all sides, forming the star points. Behind the walls were firing platforms made of earth and logs. Men could stand on these to fire over the tops of the walls with most of their bodies protected. At about eight o'clock, Prescott ordered the construction of a breastwork to run from the fort down the north side of the hill. This was simply a thick wall of earth only a few feet high that men could crouch behind as they fired at the enemy.

The British generals gathered in Governor Gage's home to discuss what to do. It was obvious that the attack they had expected to make the next morning was no longer practical. What they had to do now was to destroy or capture this fort that was a threat to the city and harbor. To the accompaniment of the steady, thunderous roar of the naval bombardment still going on, they talked over several plans.

General Howe finally presented a plan everyone was willing to accept. He suggested landing a brigade (a formation of several regiments) of troops by boat on the very tip of Charlestown peninsula, where the hills were. A small force would be sent around one side to get behind the fort, then the rest of the brigade would make a direct attack upon the fort. Howe felt sure that when the colonial soldiers saw some troops slipping around behind them and the rest coming straight at them, they would simply panic and run away. After all, how could a bunch of untrained, inexperienced farmers stand up to the onslaught of British regiments in battle formation? That was a sight that could terrify even trained professional troops of many European nations.

The British began to move quickly. Before long, drums were rattling to call the soldiers into their formations. At the water's edge, boats manned by sailors of the British navy waited to row the troops across to begin their work of destroying the American army.

Congress Adopts an Army and Picks a General

At this moment, many miles away, the new commander of that army was preparing to go to Boston. He was George Washington.

On May 10, a meeting of representatives from all the colonies had begun in Philadelphia, in the Pennsylvania colony. It was called the Continental Congress. Washington had been picked to represent Virginia at the Continental Congress. He had said good-bye to his wife, Martha, and gone to Philadelphia.

The Continental Congress had been set up to find some way of settling the differences between the colonies and the British government. But now, it had to prepare for the possibility of war with Great Britain. Because of his military experience during the French and Indian War, Washington was appointed to serve on committees dealing with ways of raising troops and getting hold of weapons and ammunition. The people he worked with were impressed by his knowledge and efficiency.

On June 14, the Congress voted to adopt the American force besieging Boston. It was named the American Continental Army. The Congress also voted to obtain more soldiers for the army. All the representatives realized the army needed a real soldier, a man with experience in warfare, to lead it. On June 15, George Washington was unanimously picked by the Congress to be the commander-in-chief of that army and all forces that might be created for the defense of the American colonies. He accepted with some reluctance, not really sure he was qualified to be the colonies' top general. ". . . I do not think myself equal to the command I am honored with," he told Congress.[4] But now, completely unaware of what was happening at Boston, he was preparing to go there to take command.

RESOLVED, THAT SIX COMPANIES OF EXPERT RIFFLEMEN [SIC], BE IMMEDIATELY RAISED IN PENNSYLVANIA, TWO IN MARYLAND, AND TWO IN VIRGINIA; THAT EACH COMPANY CONSIST OF A CAPTAIN, THREE LIEUTENANTS, FOUR SERJEANTS [SIC], FOUR CORPORALS, A DRUMMER OR TRUMPETER, AND SIXTY-EIGHT PRIVATES.

THAT EACH COMPANY . . . SHALL MARCH AND JOIN THE ARMY NEAR BOSTON, TO BE THERE EMPLOYED AS LIGHT INFANTRY, UNDER THE COMMAND OF THE CHIEF OFFICER IN THAT ARMY.

THAT THE PAY OF THE OFFICERS AND PRIVATES BE AS FOLLOWS, . . . A CAPTAIN @ 20 DOLLARS PER MONTH; A LIEUTENANT @ 13 1/3 DOLLARS; A SERJEANT @ 8 DOLLARS; A CORPORAL @ 7 1/3 DOLLARS; DRUMMER OR [TRUMPETER] @ 7 1/3 DOLL.; PRIVATES @ 6 2/3 DOLLARS; TO FIND THEIR OWN ARMS AND CLOATHS.

THAT THE FORM OF ENLISTMENT BE IN THE FOLLOWING WORDS:

I HAVE, THIS DAY, VOLUNTARILY ENLISTED MYSELF, AS A SOLDIER, IN THE AMERICAN CONTINENTAL ARMY, FOR ONE YEAR, UNLESS SOONER DISCHARGED: AND I DO BIND MYSELF TO CONFORM, IN ALL INSTANCES TO SUCH RULES AND REGULATIONS, AS ARE, OR SHALL BE, ESTABLISHED FOR THE GOVERNMENT OF THE . . . ARMY.[1]

On June 14, 1775, the Continental Congress quickly established a basic structure for the Army, as well as pay rates for officers and soldiers. However, General Washington needed to get to Boston to help these changes take effect.

THE BATTLE OF BUNKER HILL

By 11:30 on the morning of June 17, 1775, the British regiments that were to take part in the attack were marching through the streets of Boston to the wharves where boats awaited them. A British regiment was supposed to be formed of ten companies of thirty-eight men each,[2] plus officers and musicians, for a total of 477.[3] But regiments out on active service, like those in the colonies, always had far fewer men than they were supposed to. Those in Boston had only three or four hundred. Each regiment had its own particular look, so that the cuffs and lapels on the coats of the 5th Regiment, for example, were green with white trim, while those of the 23rd Regiment were dark blue trimmed with yellow.

Every regiment had two special companies: one of grenadiers and one of light infantry. Grenadiers were men chosen because they were taller and sturdier than most. They were the "special forces" troops of the regiment, used where the hardest fighting was needed. They wore helmets made of metal and bear fur, which made them look taller and showed who they were.

Top: *American soldiers pray before the Battle of Bunker Hill.* Bottom: *Colonial militiamen battle the rough roads of the Massachusetts countryside to bring powder to their fellow patriots at Bunker Hill.*

Light infantrymen were specially trained to move fast and fight mainly using their bayonets. They, too, wore a special kind of headpiece, somewhat like today's baseball cap, with the brim folded straight up.

At the wharves, the soldiers clambered into barges, some fifty men to each. Two barges were each loaded with six cannons. One after another the barges pushed off, rowed by sailors of the British Navy. As each barge reached the shore of the peninsula, the soldiers sprang out and trotted up to the crest of the little hill. There, each regiment formed its lines of battle. The cannons were hauled out of their barges and trundled into position. But when the entire force was assembled, General Howe, in command of the operation, ordered that the men be given time to eat lunch.

The Attack Begins

When he saw where the British had landed, American General Israel Putnam realized that there was a big gap in the American line of defense. Slightly to the rear of Breed's Hill was a stretch of open ground about two hundred yards wide that was totally undefended. A wooden rail fence with a stone base and a ditch in front of it ran the length of this area. Putnam ordered two hundred of his Connecticut soldiers to get behind the fence and keep the British from getting past it. He promised them reinforcements as soon as possible.

The reinforcements soon began to arrive. They had been sent from the American encampment as soon as word of the British landing was received. One group was eight hundred men from New Hampshire commanded by Colonel John Stark. Stark was another veteran of the French and Indian War. He noticed another gap in the American line—an open area about a dozen feet wide on the strip of beach between the bottom of Bunker Hill and the water. He had his men quickly pile up a low wall of stones across the beach, and get behind it in three rows. Now, there was a line of fortifications running across almost the entire width of Charlestown peninsula. In position behind it were about two thousand men and a few cannons, brought by the reinforcements.

A little before three o'clock, General Howe launched his attack according to plan. On the right, eleven companies of light infantry, about three hundred fifty men, were sent along the narrow strip of beach below Bunker Hill. Their job was to get behind the American line and swing around to strike from the rear. In the middle, two regiments, led by General Howe himself, began to march forward very slowly toward the rail fence in front of Bunker Hill. On the left, four more regiments, led by Brigadier General Robert Pigot, also began a slow march up Breed's Hill, toward the fort and breastwork.

The British Meet Unexpected Resistance

The light infantry moved in a column, twenty-three rows of men with about fifteen men in each row. Ahead, they could see the low wall of piled-up stones stretched across the beach with men crouching behind it. This did not worry them. They expected the Americans would soon run away, and then the light infantrymen would just hop over the wall and keep on going. But the troops behind the wall, Colonel Stark's New Hampshire men, did not intend to run. Farmers or not, they knew about both warfare and weapons. Many of them had fought against American Indians in the past. And they were all good shots, whose skill at hunting and shooting wild game helped keep their families fed. They crouched behind the wall in their three lines, just waiting for the redcoats to get close enough.

The light infantry came up the beach at a steady, regular marching pace. They carried their muskets upright on their shoulders, so that a bristle of bayonets gleamed above their heads. When they were about forty yards from the wall, a command was shouted. At once, the British all lowered their muskets so that the bayonets pointed straight at the Americans—a silent promise of sharp death! This was the moment when, at the sight of those oncoming blades in the hands of the finest troops in the world, the British expected the Americans to dissolve in panic and run for their lives.

Instead, there was a thunderous rippling crash of hundreds of muskets. A sheet of fire flared all along the stone wall, and a boil of thick smoke went rolling forward.

The men of Colonel Stark's first row had fired. The front two ranks of the first British company were literally flung in all directions as hundreds of lead balls smashed into them. As the soldiers of the second company came forward through the shattered bodies, Stark's second row stood up and fired, tearing more gaps in the British. The rest of the light infantry tried to keep coming, but they, too, were met by a crash of muskets, fired by Stark's third row, melting them away. Suddenly, terror struck the remaining light infantrymen. They simply turned and fled, unable to face any more of those shattering blasts of death. Ninety-six British bodies lay sprawled on the beach behind them.

The First Attack Fails

Over on the other side of the peninsula, General Pigot had also run into trouble. In order to get up Breed's Hill, his force had to go right by the edge of Charlestown—and Colonel Prescott had stationed three hundred American marksmen in the town. From behind fences and from upstairs windows the Americans opened fire. Red-coated soldiers at the ends of Pigot's lines began to go down by twos and threes. Many other soldiers halted and began firing back. The slow march toward the top of Breed's Hill came to a lurching stop.

General Pigot sent men into the town to drive the Americans out. Although they did not quite succeed, he was finally able to get his troops moving toward the fort again. Putnam, Stark, and other American officers were giving their men advice known to experienced soldiers: "Don't fire until you see the whites of their eyes."[4] With a smoothbore musket, even a skilled marksman could not be sure of hitting anything more than about fifty yards away. So, the men were being reminded to let the enemy get close enough so they could not miss.

Prescott's young farmer-soldiers waited until the British soldiers were no more than thirty yards away. Then, there was a blaze of muskets across the top of the fort and all along the breastwork. Bullets cut through the front line of sweating redcoats laboring up the steep hill burdened by fifty pounds of equipment. Some twenty went down. The British line reeled, staggered back, reformed itself, and came forward again. At twenty yards, the rebel muskets blazed again and more redcoats went down. The British began to shift rearward again, and General Pigot called a retreat.

In the center of the British army, General Howe led his two regiments toward the rail fence. The front line was made up of grenadiers in their tall, fur caps. Tough and confident, they tramped forward, sweating in the blistering heat, moving closer and closer. Suddenly, there was a crash of fire from behind the fence, and a storm of musket balls tore into the red-coated line. Men went down by threes and fours. Enclosed in thick smoke, the grenadiers left standing halted and began to fire back. Moments later, unable to see through the smoke, the men of the second rank came blundering into the grenadiers from behind. At that instant, another thundering explosion of musket fire shattered the air. More of the British were flung to the ground.

And now, just as the light infantry had done, the soldiers of General Howe's main force turned and ran.

A Second Attack

The Americans yelled in triumph. They had been attacked by the best soldiers in the world—and had made them run away.

General Howe had not been hit, but his elegant white-satin breeches were spattered with the blood of his men. He turned and walked back to the beach where his and Pigot's troops were milling about in confusion. Howe helped his officers get them into formation again. Then, once more, he led them forward. People of Boston were peering out of their upper windows and standing on the roofs of their houses. They saw the scarlet and white figures of the British start up the hill again. Hot cannonballs from the British ships had set houses in Charlestown ablaze and the whole town was now on fire. Clouds of black smoke were rolling up into the sky.

This time, the advancing line of British soldiers halted about every fifty yards to fire a volley. A number of Americans were killed or wounded. But the colonial soldiers stayed where they were and waited. When the British line was some twenty-five yards away, the Americans fired another of their shattering volleys. Once again, the red-coated lines were ripped and torn as the slashing hail of musket balls knocked men in every direction. The British tried to struggle forward and more volleys smashed into them. At last, the spectators in Boston saw the redcoats suddenly turn and flee back down the hill. They left many more motionless figures dotting the hillside behind them. The second attack had failed like the first.

General Howe Makes Another Attempt

Again, General Howe in his blood-spattered uniform was unhurt. But as he saw the second attack collapse around him, he felt, as he later admitted, a momentary surge of doubt.[5] Was it possible that the British army was actually going to fail against these colonial farmers?

Howe could not believe it—and he could not let it happen. He turned, and with musket balls whizzing around him, strode down the hill and joined the sweating, bloody, dazed troops. He called his officers together. "We will go forward once more, gentlemen," he told them.[6]

So once again, the British soldiers formed up. They moved forward in lines that stretched across almost the entire peninsula. But this time things were different. The Americans in the fort and at the rail fence had been doing a lot of shooting. Now they were just about out of bullets and powder. Some loaded their muskets with nails or small stones. Some collected rocks to throw. Many simply turned away and left the hill. They probably felt there was nothing more they could do and were glad to escape while they could.

In the fort, those still able to shoot waited until the British soldiers were no more than twenty yards away. There was a last volley. Dozens of soldiers went down.

During the Battle of Bunker Hill, British troops marched up Breed's Hill three times, taking terrible losses.

The British line wavered once more, as many men could not keep from taking two or three steps backward. But the rest continued to move forward. The others quickly caught up, and the British reached the American fort.

The Battle Comes to an End

Surging into it, the British soldiers used their bayonets savagely. They were showing their anger and frustration at having seen scores of their comrades mowed down like ripe wheat, and at having been forced to retreat twice. Most Americans had no bayonets. They tried to defend themselves by using their muskets as clubs, but thirty of them were bayoneted. A number of Americans were also shot by British soldiers.

Colonel Prescott and some others managed to fight their way out of the fort and get safely away. A few Americans still had loaded muskets, and fired shots at the British as they came swarming in. Major Pitcairn, the British officer who had been in charge at Lexington, was shot dead by an African-American soldier named Peter Salem.[7]

At the rail fence, the Americans made an orderly retreat. They backed away slowly as the British came on, those who still had ammunition firing as they went. At the stone wall on the beach, Colonel Stark's New Hampshire soldiers still had ammunition. For the third time, they shattered a British attack on their position. Finally, seeing that the rest of the American force was in retreat, they also withdrew. They left mounds of dead and wounded redcoats piled up in front of the stone wall.

What was to become known as the Battle of Bunker Hill had come to an end. The Americans went streaming back across the strip of land called the Charlestown Neck. British soldiers fired at them from behind and cannonballs bounded among them. By nightfall, the only Americans left on Breed's and Bunker Hills were thirty wounded men, unable to walk or crawl, and the stiff and silent dead.[8]

4

GEORGE WASHINGTON TAKES COMMAND

Because the American troops had been pushed off the Charlestown peninsula, most Americans regarded the Battle of Bunker Hill as a defeat. But the British generals knew better. Out of about 1,500 men, the Americans had 411 killed or wounded and thirty captured—only a little more than a quarter of their force. But 1,154 out of 2,200 redcoats had been killed or wounded in the battle. Thus, a little more than half the British force in Boston had been lost! British General Clinton wrote to a friend in England that the Battle of Bunker Hill was ". . . a dear bought victory; another such would have ruined us."[1] In his report of the battle, Governor Gage wrote that, "The loss we have sustained is greater than we can bear."[2]

George Washington also knew Bunker Hill was not a defeat for the colonial cause. Nine days after the battle, he arrived in the city of New York on the way to Boston, and received a message covering the details of the battle. Washington saw that the events on

Charlestown Peninsula showed that American colonial troops could fight off an attack by British troops, and inflict major losses on them.

Six days later, Washington arrived in the Boston area. The next morning, July 3, 1775, he officially took command of the American Continental Army—the American Army of the North American continent.

The Continental Army, including Washington, was under the orders of Congress. However, Congress was responsible for taking care of the Army's needs. Washington had left Philadelphia with instructions

In Cambridge, Massachusetts, Washington greets his troops after taking command of the American Continental Army on July 3, 1775.

from Congress. He was to do whatever needed to put the army into proper shape, build up supplies, and increase its size to about twenty thousand men by enlisting new soldiers. A man would be offered pay of twenty shillings a month to serve in the army for one year. Congress planned to pay for all this.

Washington Finds Problems

Washington went to work. The first thing he did was take a good look at his army and see how it measured up. He found many things wrong. For one, all the different sizes of regiments would lead to confusion and uncertainty in trying to plan battles and movements. For another, there was simply no discipline. The basis of an army is discipline; absolute obedience to rules and regulations and following orders instantly, without question. But most of these men, who had been farmers or workingmen, were not used to discipline. They did whatever they pleased, whenever they pleased. If an officer gave an order they did not like, they simply refused to obey it.[3] If they grew tired of being in the Army, they simply deserted—sneaked away and went home. Their living quarters were filthy and smelly. Many officers were as undisciplined as the common soldiers, and had no idea of what they were supposed to do.

Washington also found that there were serious shortages of supplies. Many men were ragged and barefoot, and some did not even have weapons. He was horrified to discover that the Army did not

THE COLONELS OR COMMANDING OFFICER OF EACH REGT. [REGIMENT] ARE ORDERED FORTHWITH, TO MAKE TWO RETURNS OF THE NUMBER OF MEN IN THEIR RESPECTIVE REGIMENTS, DISTINGUISHING SUCH AS ARE SICK, WOUNDED OR ABSENT ON FURLOUGH. AND ALSO THE QUANTITY OF AMMUNITION EACH REGIM. NOW HAS.

IT APPEARING BY THE REPORT OF HENRY WOODS, THE OFFICER OF THE MAIN GUARD, THAT ONE WILLIAM ALFRED IS CONFIN'D FOR TAKING TWO HORSES, BELONGING TO SOME PERSONS IN CONNECTICUT, BUT THAT HE HAS MADE SATISFACTION FOR THE INJURED PARTIES, WHO REQUEST THAT THEY MAY NOT BE LONGER DETAIN'D AS WITNESSES: IT IS ORDERED THAT HE BE DISCHARGED, AND AFTER RECEIVING A SEVERE REPRIMAND, BE TURNED OUT OF CAMP.

AFTER ORDERS 4 O'CLOCK P.M.

IT IS ORDERED THAT COL. GLOVER'S REGIMENT BE READY THIS EVENING . . . TO MARCH AT A MINUTES WARNING TO SUPPORT GENERAL FALSAM OF NEW HAMPSHIRE, IN CASE HIS LINES SHOULD BE ATTACK'D.

IT IS ALSO ORDER'D, THAT COL PRESCOTT'S REGIMENT EQUIP THEMSELVES, MARCH THIS EVENING AND TAKE POSSESSION OF THE WOODS LEADING TO LEECHMORES POINT, AND IN CASE OF AN ATTACK, THEN COL. GLOVER'S REGIMENT TO MARCH IMMEDIATELY TO THEIR SUPPORT.[4]

General George Washington started to issue orders immediately. These orders were dated July 3, 1775, the day that he took command.

have enough ammunition. There was only enough gunpowder for about nine shots per man.[5] But no one had done anything about this.

Washington hurled himself into the task of solving all these problems. Inefficient officers were replaced with efficient ones. To enforce discipline, he made use of a list of regulations Congress had produced for running the Army. It included rules the soldiers had to obey, and punishments they could be given if they did not. Punishment might be a fine of two month's pay or a month's imprisonment. The punishment for trying to desert was thirty-nine lashes with a whip— which kept many men from trying to desert. Discipline, health, and morale improved. More gunpowder was obtained and stocked up.

Reorganization and a Few Worries

The Army was reorganized. Regiments were formed of 8 companies of 86 men and 4 officers each, plus musicians and commanding officers, for a total of 728 men. Washington organized the regiments into three groups called divisions. Artemas Ward, Israel Putnam, and Charles Lee, who had been appointed major generals by Congress, commanded these divisions. The Continental Army became much more like an army was supposed to be.

However, one problem Washington could never quite solve was that many men simply would not stay in the Army. In Great Britain and most other European nations, being a soldier was actually a profession. A man joined an army and spent the rest of his life as a soldier, until he got too old. But this American army was very different. It was made up of groups of militia and minutemen who had agreed to be soldiers only for a few months. When their time was up, they just tramped off back to their farms or jobs. Washington was able to talk some of them into reenlisting for a few more months. But there were often times when he was faced with the sudden loss of hundreds of men from his army because their time was up. Unlike British generals, he could never count on his army having the same strength.

All the while Washington was working to solve his problems, he was deeply worried that the British would come out of Boston and attack before his army was ready for them. If the British had attacked at this time, they probably could have destroyed the American army, as Washington feared. However, the terrible losses the British had taken in the Battle of Bunker Hill had made General Howe and other officers fearful of trying to make another attack. They did not know what bad shape the Continental Army was actually in, so they simply sat in Boston, waiting for reinforcements.

Continental Reinforcements and a Plan to Invade Canada

The Continental Army was also waiting for reinforcements, and they soon began to arrive. These were men who had been recruited by Congress from the frontier regions of the colonies of Pennsylvania, Virginia, and Maryland. They were men who enjoyed living in the wilderness where they could hunt, explore, and fend for themselves. But now they had agreed to be Continental soldiers. They were armed with a gun quite different from the muskets carried by the other soldiers. Instead of the inside of the barrel being smooth, as musket barrels were, it had spiral grooves, called rifling. This caused the ball it fired to spin, which made it go straighter and farther than one fired from a musket. The gun was called a rifle. These riflemen from the frontier regions were marksmen who could hit almost anything at a distance more than three times that of a musket. They were formed into companies with names such as the First Maryland Rifles and Morgan's Rangers, commanded by Colonel Daniel Morgan. These frontier marksmen soon began striking terror into the hearts of King George III's redcoats by picking off British sentries at a distance of as much as 250 yards.

Washington not only had to think about the situation at Boston, he also had to keep an eye on military operations in the rest of the colonies. In the New England colonies and New York, there was still worry about a possible invasion from Canada. Congress hoped to prevent this by convincing the Canadians that they should side with the American colonies. However, most Canadians did not favor this.

Therefore, Congress decided that Canada should be invaded and conquered by American forces.

Morgan's Rangers soon became vital to the rebel cause. They used their specially designed rifles to shoot British soldiers from a great distance.

Washington believed this would be possible, because he knew that most of the British troops in Canada had been sent to reinforce the British force in Boston. He suggested sending two American armies into Canada, one to head for the city of Quebec and one to take the city of Montreal and then join the other at Quebec. These forces would have to be made up mainly of New York and New England militia. But to strengthen them, Washington sent some Continental Army soldiers—three companies of Morgan's Rangers with Morgan himself—to join the army headed for Quebec.

The Invasion of Canada and a Quest for Cannons

The two armies were formed and sent off. In spite of some setbacks, the one commanded by Brigadier General Richard Montgomery, about twelve hundred men, arrived outside Montreal on November 12, 1775. There were only 150 Canadian militia troops in the city, and it surrendered two days later. The other American force, commanded by Benedict Arnold, had reached Quebec on November 9. But it was in terrible shape from a tremendously difficult journey, and was down to about six hundred men. There was a force of nearly twelve hundred Canadians and some British soldiers in Quebec, so Arnold and his troops could only wait for their reinforcements to come from Montreal.

In the meantime, at Boston, Washington was struggling with a problem of artillery. The Continental Army had only a few small cannons, and many more were needed before Washington could even think of trying to make an attack to capture Boston. However, Washington knew where to get more cannons. There were 120 cannons and thousands of cannonballs in Fort Ticonderoga, which was now held by American troops. Washington sent Colonel Henry Knox, his artillery commander, and a party of artillerymen to get some of the Ticonderoga cannons and bring them back to the Continental Army.

Knox and his men reached Ticonderoga in early December. Their task was not an easy one. Most of the cannons were held in place in the fort walls with iron

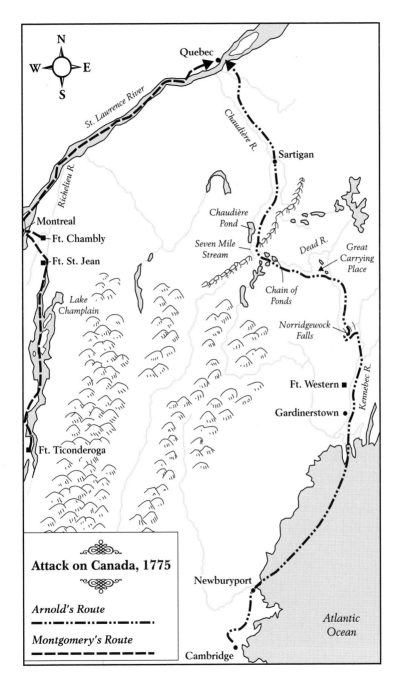

N
W ◆ E
S

Quebec

St. Lawrence River

Chaudière R.

Sartigan

Richelieu R.

Chaudière Pond

Montreal
Ft. Chambly
Ft. St. Jean

Seven Mile Stream

Dead R.

Great Carrying Place

Lake Champlain

Chain of Ponds

Norridgewock Falls

Ft. Western ■
Gardinerstown ●

Kennebec R.

Ft. Ticonderoga

Attack on Canada, 1775

Arnold's Route
— · — · —

Montgomery's Route
— — — —

Newburyport

Atlantic Ocean

Cambridge

Benedict Arnold's troops had to wait outside Quebec for Montgomery's forces to arrive from Fort Ticonderoga.

bars and concrete. Knox and his men had to break up the concrete, saw through the iron bars, and then lower each cannon to the ground with ropes, chains, and muscle-power. It was cruel, backbreaking work in a cold, snowy, New York winter.

An Assault on Quebec Fails, an Assault on Boston Begins

In Canada, Arnold's little army at Quebec was joined by Montgomery with three hundred men on December 2. Even though they were still outnumbered, the Americans attacked the city on New Year's Eve. Everything went wrong! Montgomery was killed. Arnold was shot in the leg and had to be carried away. The troops that managed to get into Quebec were cut off and captured. More than sixty Americans were killed and wounded, and 427 were taken prisoner.

At Ticonderoga, Knox and his men began the task of taking the cannons more than three hundred miles back to Cambridge. They had to be dragged over snow-covered ground and floated across ice-filled lakes and rivers on rafts, often during fierce blizzards and in below-freezing cold. Finally, in early February of 1776, Knox brought them in—fifty-five good guns plus a supply of cannonballs.

Now that he had enough artillery, Washington could proceed with his plan of attack on Boston. Just southeast of the city, projecting into Boston Harbor, was a piece of hilly land known as Dorchester Heights. Cannons put on its two biggest hills would be able to

Colonel Henry Knox's men managed to bring cannons and ammunition over snow and across icy rivers, three hundred miles from Fort Ticonderoga to the army at Boston.

bombard the British fortifications on Boston Neck, as well as Boston Harbor and Boston itself. Washington's plan was to fortify the hills, as Breed's Hill had been fortified, and fill the forts with a strong force of men and cannons. In order to keep from being shot to pieces, the British would have to attack the forts. This could be more of a bloodbath for them than the Battle of Bunker Hill had been! And while they were making a hopeless attack on the forts, Washington planned to have a strong American force land by boat in Boston and capture the city. That would leave the British cut off from their base, with no source for supplies and ammunition, and with no place to which to retreat.

Washington Springs a Surprise

But like the fortification on Breed's Hill, fortifying Dorchester Heights would have to be done secretly, in one night, so the British would not see what was happening. Carefully and quietly, night after night, troops and supplies were moved into position behind the Dorchester Heights hills. By the night of Saturday, March 2, everything was ready. George Washington gave the order.

From positions on the mainland all around Boston, dozens of American cannons suddenly began a thundering bombardment on the city. Shells exploded in the streets and balls smashed into houses.

With the arrival of morning, the American guns grew silent. They were quiet all day, but at the fall of night they opened up again, and once more kept firing until morning. These nightly artillery bombardments were actually just a diversion; an attempt to keep the British from noticing anything that might be happening on Dorchester Heights. As the guns began firing on the third night, American troops quietly moved up onto the Dorchester Heights hills. The work of building the fortifications began in the darkness. Although it was not completely finished in the morning, enough had been done so that the hills had become a strong defensive position. There were thousands of men and plenty of cannons in place behind fortifications.

It was like the Bunker Hill surprise all over again. The British suddenly saw that the Americans had constructed forts on the hills, full of soldiers and bristling with cannons. The British army in Boston was now in extreme danger. There were only two choices open to it—either attack the forts and try to capture them, or else pack up and get out of Boston by sea.

Boston is Regained

Actually, the British had already decided to evacuate Boston sometime in June, when the sailing weather would be better. But to be forced to leave now would look like a defeat. General Howe quickly worked out a plan for an attempt to capture the American fortifications and end the danger they threatened. In early morning darkness, British troops in boats would land at the bottom of Dorchester Heights. They would storm up the hill to assault the fortifications with a bayonet attack.

But on the night before the attack, a hurricane-like storm struck. It continued into the next day, lashing the sea with a fury that made it impossible for small boats to venture onto the water. However, in the driving rain and shrieking wind, the Americans on Dorchester Heights continued to work to make their defenses as unconquerable as possible.

Howe and the other generals all agreed that an attack was now out of the question. The Americans had strong fortifications, plenty of men, plenty of cannons, plenty of ammunition, and an obviously shrewd commander. The only thing the British could do was evacuate Boston.

In the following days, supplies, soldiers, and Tory citizens of Boston still loyal to King George were taken onto ships in the harbor. On the seventeenth of March 1776, nearly one hundred thirty ships, packed with some nine thousand soldiers and twelve hundred Tory civilians, moved out to sea. The siege of Boston was over. The city once again belonged to the colonials. George Washington and his Continental Army had inflicted a stinging defeat on the British.

Washington had no idea where the British ships were headed. However, he was convinced that General Howe's next move would be an attempt to capture the city of New York. It was the best seaport in the colonies and it would give the British an excellent base from

5

SETBACKS IN NEW YORK

which they could strike into the very heart of the colonies. So even before the British ships had all left Boston Harbor, Washington started part of his army moving south toward New York, and by April 4 he was heading there with the rest of his troops.

New York City today is a huge metropolis. But in 1776, it was merely a small city at the southern tip of Manhattan Island. Everything around it was mostly open countryside with woods, fields, a few farms, and some tiny villages. Washington arrived at New York on April 13 and immediately started his troops digging fortifications around the city.

The British ships had sailed for the port of Halifax, Nova Scotia, in Canada. On June 25, Washington's belief that the British intended to try to capture New York was shown to be correct. The first three vessels of a fleet of British ships from Halifax appeared in the waters of the Lower Bay, south of Manhattan Island. Within five more days there were 130 ships, and by the fifth of July, 9,300 soldiers began landing on Staten Island. Seven days later, 150 more ships arrived. This was a fleet from Britain, commanded by General Howe's brother, Admiral Richard Howe. It brought many thousands more troops, including several "hired" regiments of soldiers from Germany. This was a way for German monarchs to make money, by literally renting out their troops to fight for the army.

By this time, something of major significance had happened for the colonies. On July 2, the Continental Congress in Philadelphia had voted to declare that America no longer belonged to Great Britain. On July 4, this Declaration of Independence was announced to the world. America now regarded itself as a new, free, independent nation!

General Putnam Overlooks a Road

General Howe prepared his assault on New York. He had more than thirty thousand troops, backed up by thirty warships of the British Navy. Against this powerful force, Washington had about nineteen thousand men and, of course, no warships at all. Washington told his troops, ". . . expect an attack as soon as the wind and tide are favorable."[1] Howe's plan was to attack the American fortifications on a hilly region of Long Island known as Brooklyn Heights, just across the East River from New York City. With the forts captured, the British would be free to send troops across the river into the city.

Early on the morning of August 22, 1776, red-coated soldiers began landing on the southern coast of Long Island. By noon, fifteen thousand troops, including cavalry (soldiers on horses) and forty cannons, were ashore. Three days later, two brigades of the German troops—known as Hessians, because many of them came from the region of Germany called Hesse-Kassel—landed farther along the coast. The entire British force then moved forward toward Brooklyn Heights.

Word of the landing had quickly been sent to Washington in New York City, and he sent six regiments to bolster the forces on the Brooklyn hills. He also sent Israel Putnam to take command of the eight thousand troops there. But that was not a good choice. Putnam was completely unfamiliar with the countryside, and he made the fatal mistake of not checking things out. As a result, one road, called the Jamaica Road, which led around behind the American position, was left almost completely unguarded. Unfortunately for the Americans, the British quickly discovered this.

Howe Makes His Attack

General Howe split the British forces into two groups. With one, made up of ten thousand men, he began moving up the Jamaica Road toward the Americans' left. The other, five thousand men led by Brigadier

General Grant, advanced toward the right end of the American line. Grant's job was to quickly start pushing at the Americans and draw their attention away from the other end of their line. This worked perfectly. Shortly after midnight on the morning of August 27, groups of light infantry from Grant's force moved forward and began shooting at guards in front of the American line. General Putnam assumed that this was the start of an attack, and quickly began to rush troops there. Washington was notified at once of what was happening. He crossed the river in the middle of the night, arriving at the American position about eight o'clock in the morning. At just about 8:30, Howe's force arrived slightly behind the left end of the American troops in front of Brooklyn Heights. The British had prearranged that, at a signal, a Hessian brigade would attack the Americans from the front. At the same signal, Howe's light infantry, grenadiers, and a unit of cavalry would hit the American rear. At nine o'clock the signal was given—the booms of two cannons.

The Hessians surged forward. These German soldiers looked very different from British troops. Their coats were dark blue or dark green, and their grenadiers wore mustaches waxed to sharp points and blackened with shoe polish, to try to make themselves look fierce. They charged with a murderous bayonet attack. In some cases, they pinned American soldiers to trees with their long, sharp blades, and even stabbed wounded men and men who were trying to surrender.

They felt hatred for these "Yankees," as the British called them. They had been told that Americans scalped their prisoners and even ate them!

Howe Wins a Victory—and Makes Two Mistakes

As the Americans were trying to fight off the Hessians, they heard the sounds of British troops coming up behind them. They realized that they were caught between two forces, and scattered in panic. The American troops on the right had also been hit hard by General Grant's force. The entire American line came apart, with the men running in retreat toward the forts up on Brooklyn Heights. The Americans had two hundred men killed and wounded and nearly one thousand taken prisoner, while the British had only about four hundred killed and wounded.

Howe's plan had worked perfectly. If he had let his men keep on going, they might well have destroyed the entire American force on Long Island. But he now made a mistake. Perhaps he was afraid of having another Bunker Hill–type battle, with terrible losses if he sent his men up against the forts. At any rate, he ordered his troops to stop, begin digging trenches, and prepare to besiege the heights.

Washington had been outgeneraled and had made several mistakes. But now he took advantage of Howe's mistake. He had ordered hundreds of boats to stand by in the river in case of just such a disaster as this. Now, all through the night of August 29 and 30,

SOURCE DOCUMENT

. . . FROM THE ENEMY'S HAVING LANDED A CONSIDERABLE PART OF THEIR FORCES, AND FROM MANY OF THEIR MOVEMENTS, THERE WAS REASON TO APPREHEND [FEAR] THEY WOULD MAKE IN A LITTLE TIME A GENERAL ATTACK. AS THEY WOULD HAVE A WOOD TO PASS THROUGH BEFORE THEY COULD APPROACH THE LINES, IT WAS THOUGHT EXPEDIENT [ADVISABLE] TO PLACE A NUMBER OF MEN THERE ON THE DIFFERENT ROADS LEADING FROM WHENCE THEY WERE STATIONED, IN ORDER TO HARASS AND ANNOY THEM ON THEIR MARCH. THIS BEING DONE, EARLY THIS MORNING A SMART ENGAGEMENT ENSUED BETWEEN THE ENEMY AND OUR DETACHMENTS, WHICH, BEING UNEQUAL TO THE FORCE THEY HAD TO CONTEND WITH, HAVE SUSTAINED A PRETTY CONSIDERABLE LOSS. AT LEAST MANY OF OUR MEN ARE MISSING, AMONG THOSE THAT HAVE NOT RETURNED, ARE GENERAL SULLIVAN AND LORD STIRLING. THE ENEMY'S LOSS IS NOT KNOWN CERTAINLY; BUT WE ARE TOLD BY SUCH OF OUR TROOPS AS WERE IN THE ENGAGEMENT . . . THAT THEY HAD MANY KILLED AND WOUNDED. OUR PARTY BROUGHT OFF A LIEUTENANT, SERGEANT, AND CORPORAL, WITH TWENTY PRIVATES, PRISONERS.[2]

This excerpt from a letter by Continental Army officer Robert H. Harrison informs Congress of the outcome of the Battle of Long Island. Dated August 27, 1776, this communication was the result of a direct command from General Washington.

as silently as possible, all the American troops were taken off Long Island, across the river to New York City. With this move, Washington saved his army.

It was not until daybreak that the British discovered the Americans were gone from Brooklyn Heights. Even then, if General Howe had acted quickly, sending his troops forward at once, he could have captured many Americans before they got away. Among them would have been George Washington, because he was the very last man to get on a boat. But, once again, the English general acted too slowly and lost his chance.

Washington's foresight in having boats ready to move his troops across the East River, from Long Island to New York City, saved the Continental Army.

Washington Loses New York City

In New York City, Washington reassembled his army, knowing it was still in deadly danger. There were simply too many places where the British could land and come at the city from several sides, surrounding it and trapping the Americans. This would probably bring about the end of the war and the end of hope for America's freedom. To add to Washington's problems, the American army was also literally fading away again, as men whose enlistments were up just tramped off back to their homes and farms. Most of these men had become experienced fighters, while the few new men who came to join the army were totally inexperienced. Washington believed that such men could never stand up to the tough, skillful British soldiers in a battle.

So, he began to prepare to withdraw from New York, removing stocks of supplies, ammunition, and cannons out of the city. But before he could finish his preparations, the British attacked. At about eleven o'clock on the morning of Sunday, September 15, three warships in the East River opened up a thundering bombardment. Under cover of this, redcoats in boats landed north of the city and moved against the American entrenchments there.

As the banging of muskets began to shatter the air, Washington flung himself onto his horse and galloped to where the fighting was. To his dismay and disgust, he found that the Americans were running away. Unable to stop them, the general galloped back into

New York and organized the army's hasty withdrawal from the city. Leaving much of their supplies, ammunition, and many cannons behind, the Americans moved northward to a hilly region known as Harlem Heights, where entrenchments had been dug. The city of New York was now completely in British hands.

A Tiny Victory, Another Defeat

The next day, September 16, Washington sent a force of about one hundred fifty men to try to find out what the British might be up to. The Americans ran into a strong force of several hundred British light infantry and Scottish troops, some of the toughest fighters in the British Army. The American commander pulled his men back to keep from being surrounded. Hearing the sound of musket fire, Washington galloped down to see what was happening. The Americans were slowly dropping back, exchanging shots with the enemy.

Washington sent for reinforcements and ordered a counterattack. While a force of about one hundred fifty Americans began to advance slowly toward the British, another force moved around the enemy's right side to cut them off. Becoming aware of this, the British began to pull back. But they, too, began to receive reinforcements. Not wanting to become involved in a major battle, Washington ordered his troops back to Harlem Heights. He had lost 120 men killed and wounded, while Howe had lost 270.[3] This little battle became known as the Battle of Harlem Heights, a tiny American victory. But it showed that

Continental troops could beat the British in the open, and not just when they were behind fortifications. It boosted American morale.

Once again, General Howe became cautious, making no moves for nearly a month. Then, he made two attempts to slip troops around the side of Harlem Heights. These were beaten off, but Washington decided the position was too insecure. He marched his troops north to the town of White Plains. There, he strung his soldiers out on another line of hills.

With his British and Hessian army, which had now been reinforced by about four thousand more Hessians, Howe moved in pursuit. On October 28, he sent his forces up the wooded hills in an attack. The British and Hessians took heavier casualties—231 men—but forced the Americans off the hills with a loss of 130 men and 34 cannons left behind.[4]

Washington Plays Hide-and-Seek

On the first of November, Howe attacked again. But once more he had moved too slowly. Washington's army had slipped away northward, to a stronger position. Washington now split the American forces up in order to keep better watch over British movements. Leaving about six thousand men in New York under command of Major General Charles Lee, he took four thousand to Newark, New Jersey. Howe sent General Charles Cornwallis after him with about four thousand men, but again Washington slipped away. He took his troops across the Delaware River into the colony of

Pennsylvania. Washington had now slipped away from the British so many times that they had nicknamed him "the Old Fox." He was like a sly fox that could skillfully escape a pack of hounds trying to catch it. Cornwallis did not follow Washington, but he put small forces in a number of towns along the Delaware River in New Jersey, to keep watch in case the Americans tried to come back.

It was now well into December, and things had gone badly for American forces for most of the year 1776. The attack against the Canadian province of Quebec by Arnold had been a disaster, with a serious loss of men and equipment. He had been forced to retreat to Montreal. In New York, Washington's army had won a tiny victory at Harlem Heights, but had been pushed out of New York City, and had lost the battles of Long Island and White Plains. Two important forts with twenty-eight hundred men and many cannons, supplies, and ammunition had also been lost. Many Americans were beginning to fear that their cause was hopeless and that the powerful military forces of Great Britain were slowly going to crush American independence.

Washington felt the revolution needed a victory or it would simply wither away. He decided to strike at one of the small forces Cornwallis had left along the Delaware River in New Jersey. The plan he came up with was one of the most daring and dangerous of the entire Revolutionary War.

6

SOME VICTORIES AND A SERIOUS DEFEAT

Howe had left the town of Trenton, New Jersey, in the hands of three Hessian regiments under the command of German Colonel Johann Rall. From his spies, Washington learned this man was a brawling drunkard who regarded the Continental Army with contempt. He did not even bother to take precautions to safeguard his men from attack. Washington believed the Hessians could be caught by surprise, and planned an attack on Trenton. He scheduled it for the day after Christmas. He knew it was a German custom to celebrate Christmas very heartily, and the German soldiers might be tired and not feeling well the next day. But to get to Trenton, the army would have to cross the Delaware River, and Washington had no boats. However, New Jersey men in Washington's army knew where boats were kept for miles around. He sent a group of them on a secret mission to steal the boats that were needed! By December 20, they had brought back twenty-six.

On Christmas Day, a wild storm whipped over the area. At eleven o'clock that night, Washington's soldiers began crossing the ice-filled Delaware in freezing sleet, howling wind, and bone-chilling cold. Then, they marched nine miles through a forest to reach Trenton. Most of the men were in ragged, thin clothing and many actually did not even have shoes. They left bloody footprints in the icy snow.[1]

A Dazzling Victory

Washington had about twenty-four hundred men and eighteen cannons. They were in two divisions, one

On Christmas night, 1776, Washington's troops crossed the ice-filled Delaware River in boats, to make a surprise attack on the British-held town of Trenton, New Jersey. This depiction of Washington's crossing was painted by Emanuel Leutze in 1851.

commanded by Major General Nathanael Greene, the other commanded by Major General John Sullivan. Five miles from Trenton, Washington put the divisions on two different roads so that one could hit Trenton from the north and the other from the west.

At about eight o'clock in the morning, Greene's division, with which Washington had stayed, emerged from the forest at the edge of the town. Just then, a Hessian officer stepped out of a house and saw them. He shouted out an alarm. Seventeen soldiers came rushing out of the house, fired a wild volley that hit no one and fled into the town, yelling. Washington had been right about the Germans over-celebrating Christmas. Colonel Rall had gotten so drunk that his men had to carry him to bed, and now he came lurching out of his house half-dazed. Most of the Hessian soldiers were not in much better shape. Tired and still half-drunk, they staggered into the streets, trying to form into lines for battle.

American cannons were hauled forward to where they could fire down the streets. Cannonballs began to slam into the Hessians, flinging them about like torn and bloody bowling pins. General Sullivan's troops came charging into the town from the west, shooting as they came. Colonel Rall struggled onto his horse and tried to lead a doomed and useless charge against the American infantry and cannons. He went down with two horrible wounds in his body, and died. Hessians began to throw down their muskets and raise their hands in surrender. The brightly colored flags of

The attack on Trenton, New Jersey, was a magnificent success. The Hessian regiment holding the town had some 40 men killed and wounded, and the remaining 918 surrendered. The Continental Army had only two men killed and three wounded.

the German regiments were lowered to the ground, also indicating surrender. The battle was over. The Hessians had 40 men killed or wounded and 918 taken prisoner.[2] Two Americans had been killed and three wounded. It was a dazzling victory for American forces.

The British Come Looking for Washington

But Washington was now faced with a serious problem. On January 1, the enlistments of most of his men

I CROSSED OVER TO JERSEY THE EVENING OF THE 25TH. ABOUT 9 MILES ABOVE TRENTON WITH UPWARDS OF 2000 MEN AND ATTACKED THREE REGIMENTS OF HESSIANS, CONSISTING OF 1500 MEN ABOUT 8 O'CLOCK NEXT MORNING. OUR MEN PUSHED ON WITH SUCH RAPIDITY, THAT THEY SOON CARRIED FOUR PIECES OF CANNON OUT OF SIX, SURROUNDED THE ENEMY, AND OBLIGED 30 OFFICERS AND 886 PRIVATES TO LAY DOWN THEIR ARMS WITHOUT FIRING A SHOT. OUR LOSS WAS ONLY TWO OFFICERS AND TWO OR THREE PRIVATES WOUNDED. THE ENEMY HAD BETWEEN 20 AND 30 KILLED. WE SHOULD HAVE MADE THE WHOLE OF THEM PRISONERS, COULD GENL. EWING HAVE PASSED THE DELAWARE AT TRENTON AND GOT IN THEIR REAR, BUT THE ICE PREVENTED HIM. . . .

YOUR SON WAS MENTIONED AMONG THE FIRST OF OUR PRISONERS THAT I DEMANDED IN EXCHANGE; BUT GENL. HOWE . . . SENT OUT OTHERS THAN THOSE I DEMANDED. I HAVE REMONSTRATED [PROTESTED] TO HIM UPON THIS HEAD, AND HAVE ASSURED HIM THAT I WILL SEND IN NO MORE PRISONERS TILL HE SENDS OUT THE PAROLES OF THE OFFICERS TAKEN IN CANADA.[3]

In this letter to Major-General Alexander McDougall, Washington describes the events at Trenton. (Washington actually underestimates the number of Hessian casualties.) He also informs McDougall on the status of his prisoner-of-war son.

would be up, and they would leave for home. He would have only a few hundred men left.

Washington called his entire army together. He made a speech, begging the men to reenlist. His willingness to keep fighting for America's freedom inspired them and most agreed. The Continental Army remained in existence!

News of the loss of Trenton reached New York several days later. General Howe immediately ordered General Cornwallis to go and put a stop to Washington's tricks once and for all. Cornwallis hurried to the town of Princeton, New Jersey, where a number of British regiments were stationed, and put together an army of about seven thousand men. Before dawn on the morning of January 2, this army set out on the eleven-mile march to Trenton.

At about ten o'clock the British were still several miles from Trenton when there was the sudden sharp crack of a rifle. A Hessian toppled from his horse, dead. More shots rang out. Cornwallis's men realized that they were under fire from American riflemen hiding among the trees on each side of the road. The riflemen had been sent there by Washington. A man had ridden from Princeton to tell him the British were coming and had left a small rearguard and a large amount of supplies in the town. Armed with this information, Washington and his top officers had worked out a plan. He now had about five thousand reinforcements. He put most of them in position behind the little Assunpink Creek, which joined the

Delaware River just behind Trenton. Then, he sent out a small group of riflemen to delay the British advance. The riflemen fought just as the minutemen had at Concord, firing at the marching British from behind trees and other cover. They slowed the British down so much that Cornwallis did not reach Trenton and the creek until dark.

The "Old Fox" Springs Another Surprise

Cornwallis ordered his men to encamp, and confidently prepared to attack across the creek first thing in the morning. He felt sure that Washington had gotten his army caught in a trap from which it could not escape. He did not think the Americans could make it across the Delaware River. It was now so choked with ice that boats could not move upon it, but it was not solid enough so that men could march across it, either. And the Americans could not simply pull back, because there was nowhere for them to go. "We've got the old fox safe now," Cornwallis said, smugly. "We'll go over and bag him in the morning."[4]

But Washington was not trapped. There had been plenty of time to check out all the side roads in the area that the British would not know about, and Washington's plan made use of this. He was not going to stay behind Assunpink Creek—he was going to take his army up a side road to Princeton!

In the winter darkness, campfires glowed on both sides of the creek. As long as British sentries saw fires still burning on the American side, with men moving among them, they were sure that the Continental troops were there. But at about one o'clock, the Americans began to slip away up a side road. The men moved as silently as possible. The wheels of cannons and wagons were wrapped with rags to muffle their sound. A few hundred men stayed behind for a while, keeping the fires going, and letting themselves be seen so the British sentries would not suspect anything. Then they, too, gradually slipped away, a few at a time. Thus, in the morning, as Cornwallis and his officers looked across the creek they saw only smoldering fires, with everyone and everything gone.

Cornwallis realized that he had been outwitted. Then, the sound of booming cannons came drifting on the wind, faint and far away. Cornwallis knew that Washington's army was now behind him, attacking Princeton!

Another American Victory

The Americans had bumped into the British rearguard just outside Princeton. There was a brisk battle that lasted only forty-five minutes, and at one point the Americans were on the edge of a disastrous defeat. But they managed to rally, turning the tables, and shattered the British, sending them fleeing in all directions. Watching this, Washington gleefully yelled out, "It's a fine fox chase, boys!"[5]

The Americans gathered up as much of the British supplies as they could, burned and destroyed most of the rest, then marched away. American losses were

40 men killed and wounded; the British had about 86 killed and wounded, and had about 187 men taken prisoner.

Cornwallis hurried to Princeton, hoping to catch up to Washington, but could not do so. The Americans had headed north to Morristown. Cornwallis went back to New York, and General Howe ordered all British troops out of New Jersey except for strong forces left in two towns close to the New York colony border. At Morristown, the ragged, shivering, half-starved men of Washington's army built log huts and settled down to try to get warm and nourished.

Washington had given the revolution the victories it needed to keep going. His army of poorly clothed, poorly fed, poorly equipped, and untrained farmers and workmen had defeated some of the world's most highly regarded soldiers. He had liberated most of New Jersey. British forces had been within nineteen miles of what was then the American capital, Philadelphia. Now, Washington had pushed them back almost sixty miles. Throughout America, people who had feared the revolution was doomed rejoiced. In Britain, there was concern.

Aid From France, Threats From the British

Other nations also recognized the importance of the American victories. The kingdom of France had been watching the American Revolution with great interest. France and Great Britain were bitter enemies. They had fought three major wars against each other since the beginning of the 1700s. France would be delighted to see Great Britain lose all its American colonies. Now that America had declared its independence and had gained some victories, the French government decided to help it. Early in 1777, France began secretly providing the American rebels with military supplies— cannons, muskets, powder and ammunition, blankets, uniforms, and shoes. Much of this badly needed equipment was eventually delivered to George Washington's army. As months passed, the army became better clothed, healthier, and more confident.

Meanwhile, the British were beginning to strike back to get even for Trenton and Princeton. In early July, a British and Hessian army of about seven thousand men, commanded by Major General Burgoyne, moved down out of Canada. It captured Fort Ticonderoga from the tiny American force that held it and marched into upper New York. On July 23, 260 ships sailed from New York City carrying fifteen thousand British and Hessian soldiers under the command of General Howe himself.

Washington was concerned about Burgoyne's movements in New York. But he was more concerned about what Howe was up to. He felt sure that Howe was going to attempt to capture Philadelphia, where Congress was. Washington's army now numbered eleven thousand men, and he sent several hundred men, with Generals Arnold and Benjamin Lincoln, to reinforce the American militia forces in upper New

York. He started the rest marching into Pennsylvania, toward Philadelphia.

A Militia Victory in New York; Howe Comes to Pennsylvania

In Philadelphia, Washington met a man who had come all the way from France to volunteer for service in the Continental Army. He was the Marquis de Lafayette, a twenty-year-old nobleman and captain in the French Army who wanted to fight against the British. Congress had appointed him a major general. Washington took the young Frenchman on as a member of his staff.

While Washington waited to find out where Howe was going, things began to happen in New York and New England. For one thing, on August 4, Congress appointed Major General Horatio Gates as commander of American troops in New York. As Gates was traveling to New York, Burgoyne sent a small force of about eight hundred British and German troops on a raiding expedition for horses. On August 16—near Bennington, Vermont, but still in New York—they were ambushed by an American army of fifteen hundred militiamen, and a few hundred Continentals. The militiamen were commanded by John Stark, one of the heroes of Bunker Hill. "We'll beat them before night, or Molly Stark will be a widow!" Stark declared grimly.[6] Burgoyne's troops were scattered and many were captured. Another force of six hundred British troops sent to help them was also overwhelmed.

Burgoyne lost almost a thousand men to less than one hundred Americans killed or wounded.[7] The Battle of Bennington, as it came to be called, was a resounding American victory.

On August 23, Howe's ships finally showed up in Chesapeake Bay, the long finger of water that reaches out of the Atlantic Ocean up through the middle of Maryland, nearly to the edge of Pennsylvania. Washington had been right: Howe did intend to capture Philadelphia. The British ships dropped anchor at the top of the bay. The troops disembarked and marched out of Maryland into Pennsylvania, heading toward Philadelphia, some fifty miles away.

The Battle of Brandywine—A Defeat But Not a Disaster

Washington was quickly notified. On August 24, he marched his army to a stream known as Brandywine Creek, flowing through the countryside between Philadelphia and the advancing British forces. Most of the Brandywine was deep, with high banks. But there were a number of fords—places where the water was shallow enough for men and horses to wade across. Washington arranged his forces to cover all the fords on a long stretch of the creek where he thought the British were most likely to try to cross in order to reach Philadelphia.

By September 10, Howe's army was five miles from Brandywine Creek. The next morning, he split his forces. He sent five thousand men under Hessian

Washington was caught by surprise in the Battle of Brandywine, and the Continental Army could have been destroyed. But the Army held together to fight again.

General von Knyphausen toward the fording place across the creek known as Chad's Ford. Howe and General Cornwallis took the rest of the army farther north along the creek. The plan was for Von Knyphausen to attract the Americans' attention with an attack at Chad's Ford. Meanwhile, the main British force would cross the creek much farther up, where there were no American troops. They would then move down to hit Washington's line from the flank.

Von Knyphausen's men moved against Chad's Ford at mid-morning and began bombarding Americans across the creek with cannon fire. The troops of Howe and Cornwallis crossed the creek by one o'clock in the afternoon. They formed up into lines of attack and marched against Washington's flank. Caught by surprise and outnumbered, the Americans at that end of the line began to give way. Washington sent troops from another part of the line to help them. But then, von Knyphausen attacked across Chad's Ford, shattering the American line there. The entire line began to come apart and Washington had to order a withdrawal to save the army.

Once again, Washington had been outgeneraled by Howe. His army had lost some 1,300 killed, wounded, or captured, and had failed to stop the British, who lost only 583 men.[8] However, the Continental Army was still intact. On September 26, troops of Howe's army marched into Philadelphia. The American capital had been captured.

7

REBUILDING AN ARMY

Things had not gone well in Pennsylvania, but in New York they were going much better. General Gates had arrived and had ordered fortifications built in an area through which Burgoyne's army would have to pass. On September 19, 1777, Burgoyne attacked this position and suffered terrible casualties from Daniel Morgan's riflemen and a counterattack by several regiments led by Benedict Arnold. The British lost about six hundred men to the Americans' slightly more than three hundred. Burgoyne's army was melting away.

The capture of Philadelphia did not really mean much to the revolution. Before the British arrived, Congress simply moved to the town of York, some eighty miles away, and went right on with its business. But the loss of the city he had marched his army many miles to protect was a humiliating defeat for Washington.[1] He looked for a way to make up for it.

General Howe was keeping only part of his army in Philadelphia. He had put most of it, about nine thousand men, in a community called Germantown, eight miles away. Washington's army was outnumbered by the British force at Germantown, and he knew Howe would never expect him to attack there. So, that was exactly what he decided to do.

He started his troops moving toward Germantown at seven o'clock on the night of October 3. They reached the edge of the town at just about dawn the next morning. While the sun was rising, a thick fog settled over the area. Soon, Washington's men could see no farther than about thirty yards. As they moved slowly forward, they ran into a British regiment. Flashes of light began to flicker throughout the fog as men fired at dim shapes in front of them. The British began to pull back.

A Stunning British Defeat, a Striking French Decision

The American attack was going well when something abruptly went wrong. Two American units blundered into each other in the fog and opened fire, each thinking the other was a British force. The noise and confusion caused a general panic, and many soldiers began to run away. With his army beginning to dissolve, Washington had no choice but to order buglers to sound the call to withdraw. The Continental Army had 673 casualties and about 400 men captured to only about 535 British casualties. Yet, the Battle of Germantown actually became a kind of victory for Washington and his army. Washington had again shown he was daringly bold, and people throughout

America, as well as in other countries, admired him for it.

Four days later, something happened at Saratoga, New York, that was a turning point in the Revolutionary War. The army of General Burgoyne again moved against General Gates's American force, and again was badly beaten. Burgoyne lost 600 men while Gates lost only 150. Burgoyne's army was now less than five thousand, and it was running out of food and ammunition. He sent a message to Gates asking to talk over terms of surrender. A whole British army was out of the war.

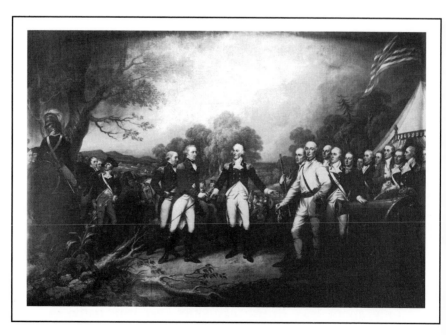

British general John Burgoyne surrenders at Saratoga. Because it helped gain the support of France, the battle marked a turning point in the Revolutionary War.

Word of the Battle of Saratoga reached France on December 4. The French government had been trying to decide whether to strike at Great Britain by officially acknowledging America as an independent nation. Now, the news of Burgoyne's surrender as well as of Washington's daring attack at Germantown brought France to a decision. On December 17, the French government announced that it now considered the United States a new nation, no longer part of Great Britain. This was an insult to the British, and it meant that France and Great Britain would soon be at war— a tremendous boost for the American cause.

The Winter That Changed the Continental Army

On December 11, with winter's cold settling over the land, Washington's army had headed to where it would spend the winter months—Valley Forge, Pennsylvania. This was a small open area surrounded by thick forest. It was only twenty miles from Philadelphia, where the British army was spending its winter, enjoying snug warmth and good food. But Washington's ragged, poorly fed soldiers slept in cloth tents while they chopped trees, trimmed logs, and built huts to live in. This work was not finished until mid-January.

Now, Washington was joined by one of the strangest heroes of the Revolutionary War, the man known as Baron Friedrich Wilhelm Ludolf Gerhard Augustin von Steuben. He was not really a baron—he just called himself that to get greater respect. However,

The Continental Army suffered from freezing temperatures, sickness, and lack of food during the winter of 1777 at Valley Forge. Here, Washington stands with Lafayette (left) among cold and tired soldiers.

he really had been an officer in the army of the German kingdom of Prussia. The Prussian Army was one of the best in Europe, and Von Steuben was an expert in methods of Prussian-style warfare—rigid discipline and training that made a soldier able to fire four or five shots a minute. He came to America in December of 1777 and was taken before Congress where he offered to serve as an unpaid volunteer in the American army, training the troops. He was accepted and sent to Valley Forge on February 23, 1778. With Washington's approval, he began his training program in March.

Von Steuben started with one hundred men. He understood no English, but spoke in French, which an American officer translated. Daily, he drilled and drilled the Americans, teaching them how to move together simultaneously and obey commands instantly, without confusion or hesitation. He often yelled at them in a mixture of German, French, and broken English to make them work harder. He showed them how to cut down the number of moves needed to load and fire a musket, so they could do these things faster than British soldiers could. He made the men confident in themselves and confident that they could fight the British on equal terms. When he felt his hundred men were perfect, he began with another hundred.

Meanwhile, the men he had first trained were all showing others what they had learned. In this way, Von Steuben's teachings spread rapidly through the Army. Extremely impressed, Washington requested

At Valley Forge, the former Prussian officer, Baron von Steuben, used Prussian Army methods to teach the inexperienced Americans how to become efficient and effective soldiers.

that Congress appoint Von Steuben a major general in the Continental Army, with pay.

American Spirits Rise, British Spirits Sink

The winter months at Valley Forge were a period of extreme suffering for the soldiers of Washington's army. Many of them were so raggedly clothed that they were practically naked. They could not leave their huts for fear of freezing to death in the open. There were many deaths during the winter from diseases made worse by exposure, lack of food, and lack of medical supplies. Washington did everything he could for his men. He begged Congress for help, sent out groups of soldiers to scour the countryside for food and clothing and wrote to the governors of all the surrounding states. But conditions remained extremely bad.

However, the men who went through the winter at Valley Forge were the heart of the Continental Army. They were men who believed deeply in making the United States free. And they all had deep faith in their commander, George Washington.

Their spirits began to rise as weather warmed and trees turned pale green, announcing the arrival of spring, 1778. They rose higher when, on May 7, word reached Valley Forge that France, with its large, powerful army and navy, was sending troops and ships to America, to help fight the British.

In British-occupied Philadelphia, the mood was grim. The British knew they could not stay there. They would be in danger of being trapped between

THE MELANCHOLY PROSPECT BEFORE US, WITH RESPECT TO SUPPLIES OF PROVISIONS, INDUCES ME, RELUCTANTLY TO TROUBLE YOU ON A SUBJECT, WHICH DOES NOT NATURALLY FALL WITHIN THE CIRCLE OF YOUR ATTENTION.

THE SITUATION . . . OF THE ARMY . . . IS MORE DEPLORABLE, THAN YOU CAN EASILY IMAGINE. WE HAVE FREQUENTLY SUFFERED TEMPORARY WANT AND GREAT INCONVENIENCES, AND FOR SEVERAL DAYS PAST, WE HAVE EXPERIENCED LITTLE LESS THAN FAMINE IN CAMP; AND HAVE HAD MUCH CAUSE TO DREAD A GENERAL MUTINY AND DISPERSION. OUR FUTURE PROSPECTS ARE, IF POSSIBLE, STILL WORSE: THE [AMMUNITION AND POWDER] MAGAZINES LAID UP, AS FAR AS MY INFORMATION REACHES, ARE INSIGNIFICANT, TOTALLY INCOMPETENT TO OUR NECESSITIES, AND FROM EVERY APPEARANCE, THERE HAS BEEN HERETOFORE SO ASTONISHING A DEFICIENCY IN PROVIDING, THAT UNLESS THE MOST VIGOROUS AND EFFECTUAL MEASURES ARE AT ONCE, EVERY WHERE [SIC] ADOPTED, THE LANGUAGE IS NOT TO STRONG TO DECLARE, THAT WE SHALL NOT BE ABLE TO MAKE ANOTHER [MILITARY] CAMPAIGN.[2]

In this excerpt from a February 19, 1778 appeal, Washington describes the conditions at Valley Forge to Patrick Henry, the current governor of Virginia. He later goes on to ask Henry for help. Henry sent cattle to Valley Forge and, throughout the war, made sure his colony supplied its own soldiers with clothes and shoes.

Washington's army and French forces moving up through Delaware. General Howe had returned to England, and General Sir Henry Clinton was now commander of British forces in America. On June 16, he started moving his troops out of Philadelphia toward New Jersey.

Washington Challenges the British Army

Washington had been waiting for this movement of the British troops. His army was in better shape now, and was ready to meet the British in battle. Clinton's army was the largest British force in the United States, and if the Continental Army could defeat it, the war might end and America would be victorious.

But it was necessary to be cautious. If the American army should be defeated, the revolution could collapse. Washington called a meeting of his top officers to discuss how to proceed. His second-in-command, General Charles Lee, urged that the British should just be allowed to leave without being attacked. But most of the other generals wanted to at least cause the enemy some trouble. It was finally decided that a small force of about four thousand men, under Lee, should follow the British closely, watching for a chance to do whatever damage they could without too much risk. The rest of the army, under Washington, would follow at a distance, ready to move forward quickly.

On the morning of June 28, the start of one of the hottest days of the year, Clinton's army was encamped around Monmouth Court House. General Lee's small force was encamped some five miles away. Early in the morning, most of the British began to march away. A strong force was left behind for a time, to guard against anything Lee might try. Lee ordered an attack on this force, hoping to cut it off from joining the rest of the British, and wiping it out or capturing it. But hearing the sound of cannons and muskets, Clinton turned his army around and marched back. He hoped to force the American troops into a major battle and destroy them.

Washington Takes Charge

It quickly became obvious that Lee had not planned for this and had not given clear orders about what to do. The American troops got mixed up with one another and began to fall back. Lee hastily ordered a retreat. The Americans began to stream toward the rear with the British moving quickly up behind them.

Learning what was happening, Washington brought his forces quickly forward. Encountering Lee, he angrily asked why the troops were retreating. "What is the meaning of this, sir?" he demanded.[3] Lee replied that he did not think American troops could stand against a British bayonet attack. Washington shouted a calculated insult and snapped, ". . . you never tried them!"[4] Riding from place to place, he managed to halt the retreat. He got the American forces into line behind a shallow ravine studded with patches of woods. There, they awaited the assault of the oncoming redcoats.

The battle that followed, known as the Battle of Monmouth, was fought in blistering heat that reached 100 degrees. The British struck at the left end of the American line, with a charge of light infantry and Scottish troops. Loading and firing as Von Steuben had taught them, men of the New Hampshire and Virginia regiments cut down the attackers with rapid volleys of well-aimed fire. The British fell back.

Next, Clinton threw a strong attack against the right end of the American line with some of his best troops. They, too, were driven back by murderous fire. Even while that attack was taking place, Clinton hurled another attack at the center of the line, where General "Mad" Anthony Wayne was in command. A wave of

At the Battle of Monmouth, American musket fire and counterattacks stopped every British charge.

British grenadiers in their tall black fur caps came swiftly at the Americans with their bayonets bristling before them.

The British Army Meets Its Equal

"Steady, steady," General Wayne told his men. "Wait for the word. . . ."[5] The Americans stood firm as the grenadiers drew close enough for their squinted eyes and clenched teeth to be clearly seen. Then, at Wayne's command, there was a blast of muskets that practically wiped the grenadiers away. This British attack, too, had failed!

It was after five o'clock by this time, and the heat was still intense. With parched lips and dry throats, the men of both armies were suffering horribly from thirst. Clinton pulled his entire army back half a mile and the Americans were simply too exhausted and thirsty to follow. Many actually collapsed where they stood. Each side had lost about 350 men; nearly a hundred of them had died of sunstroke or heat exhaustion.

Darkness finally settled over the battlefield. Around midnight, moving very quietly, the British army formed up and trudged away.

Up until now, British generals had always welcomed the chance for an open battle against American forces that were not in fortified positions, because they always felt sure of winning. There had been several times when Washington's army had been forced to slip away during a night rather than fight a British force that could undoubtedly beat it. But now it was the British who had slipped away in darkness.

Clinton had tried to shatter Washington's army in open battle, but had found that the Americans now had the discipline and skill that made them a match for the British. There was an even chance that if battle resumed the next morning, the British would be defeated. Rather than take a risk, Clinton removed his army from the field of battle.

Clinton took his army to New York City. Washington followed, and positioned his troops around the city, bottling the British up. It was like the siege of Boston all over again. The British position was too strong for the Americans to risk trying to break in, the American

VICTORY IN VIRGINIA

force was too strong for the British to risk trying to break out. So, in the northern colonies, except for some small attacks to capture forts, the war came to a standstill.

However, the British now began to think about the South—the colonies of Virginia, Georgia, and North and South Carolina. There were a great many Tory loyalists in the South, and the British government believed they might be willing to help fight the rebels.

In November of 1778, Clinton sent a force of thirty-five hundred men south by ship. They landed near the seaport of Savannah in the Georgia colony, and marched on the city. A small force of about eight hundred fifty Georgia militiamen was quickly thrown together to try to stop them.[1] But the British shattered these militia troops and captured Savannah on

December 29. The Americans had 94 casualties and
453 captured, while the British lost only 26 men.[2]
Loyalists flocked to join the British, and a month later
a British and loyalist force captured the important river
town of Augusta. It began to look as if Georgia was
being cut loose from the United States!

This was a serious situation. Major General
Benjamin Lincoln was in command of American operations in the South, at the seaport of Charleston,
South Carolina, with a small force of mostly militiamen. In the spring of 1779, Washington sent
him twenty-five hundred Continental soldiers. This
gave Lincoln about fifty-five hundred troops. In
September, he took them into Georgia to join four
thousand French troops that had landed near Savannah
by a French fleet. Together, they made an attack on the
British force in the city. It was a dismal failure. The
French took some 700 casualties, the Americans 450,
the British fewer than 150.[3] The French fleet and soldiers sailed off and Lincoln's troops trudged back to
Charleston.

A Bitter Surrender, a Difficult Time, a Welcome Arrival

On the day after Christmas, General Clinton himself
sailed south with eighty-five hundred men. On
February 11, 1780, he landed this force thirty miles
south of Charleston. Not wanting to get trapped,
General Lincoln prepared to pull out of Charleston.
But the politicians in charge of the city demanded that

he defend it. Clinton's army arrived, surrounded the city, and began to bombard it with cannon fire. After weeks of bombardment, Lincoln decided he had to surrender. Thus, the largest American army in the South, which included more than two thousand Continentals, was captured.

In Morristown, New Jersey, where it had spent the winter, the Continental Army was having a very difficult time. The conditions were nearly as bad as those at Valley Forge had been. Congress had no money and the soldiers were underfed, dressed in rags, unpaid, and many were deserting. Washington was down to only thirty-five hundred men.

However, on July 10, a French fleet of twelve warships arrived at the port of Newport, Rhode Island. They brought six thousand French troops, commanded by the Comte de Rochambeau. This was a force that had been sent to link up with the Continental Army to go on the offensive against the British. Like the British soldiers, these men were professionals, who were well-trained, well-equipped, and well-clothed. Americans were impressed by their all-white uniforms, with touches of color such as pale blue lapels, and red cuffs, to identify each regiment.

In the south, General Clinton had sailed back to New York leaving Cornwallis in command. Against Washington's wishes, Congress had appointed General Horatio Gates commander of all American forces in the South. In late August, Gates was in South Carolina with about forty-one hundred men when Cornwallis came to meet him in open battle.

A Shameful Defeat, a Bitter Betrayal, an Important Change

The two armies came together on August 16, 1780, near Camden, South Carolina. As the British began to attack, the militia units forming part of the American line collapsed in panic and ran—and Gates fled with them on horseback. The Continental regiments left were hit from all sides. The American army dissolved, losing about nine hundred, with a thousand men taken prisoner. British casualties were about 418.

This was bitter news, but there was more bitter news to come. In September, Washington was stunned to learn that Benedict Arnold had turned traitor to the United States. Arnold felt that he had never been properly rewarded for his service to the American cause, and had gone over to the British side. "Arnold has betrayed us," Washington exclaimed. "Whom can we trust now?"[4]

Disgusted by General Gates's actions at the Battle of Camden, Congress asked Washington to appoint a new commander for American forces in the South. He named Nathanael Greene.

Greene took command of the little army of about fifteen hundred men in South Carolina on December 2, 1780. He decided to simply try to keep Cornwallis uncertain of what he might do. He split his army into two forces and put one on each side of Winnsboro, where Cornwallis was encamped. Thus, if Cornwallis were to try to attack either American force, the other could hit him from the rear.

As 1781 began, Cornwallis decided he had better do something about the American troops on each side of him. He sent Lieutenant Colonel Banastre Tarleton, with about eleven hundred men to destroy one force while he kept watch on the other.

The force Tarleton was supposed to destroy was commanded by Daniel Morgan, who had made careful plans. His men were in a good defensive position in a hilly area known as Cowpens, some of them hidden. Morgan told the militiamen who were with him to just ". . . give them three fires (volleys). . . ." and that would do the job.[5]

A Win in South Carolina, Bright Prospects in Virginia

Tarleton attacked on the morning of January 17. His infantry was shattered by the militiamen's volleys and his cavalry was wiped out by a charge of American cavalry, launched from behind a hill. The British had more than three hundred men killed and wounded, and nearly six hundred captured. The Americans had only twelve killed and sixty wounded.

Cowpens was a rousing American victory that brought men flocking to Greene's army. On March 15, Cornwallis attacked him at Guilford Court House, in North Carolina. After some bitter fighting that cost Greene 261 casualties, he felt he had to retreat. But he had given Cornwallis 532 casualties, and the American army was still in good shape. Greene began fighting small battles from which he always retreated, but always gave the British more casualties than he took. "We fight, get beat, rise, and fight again," he commented.[6]

On May 20, leaving a small force to keep watch on Greene, Cornwallis went into Virginia with an army of seventy-two hundred men. Entirely on his own, without orders from Clinton, he had decided to capture Virginia. This would split the North and South apart with British-controlled territory between them, giving the British a tremendous advantage. In February, Washington had sent the Marquis de Lafayette into Virginia with twelve hundred Continental Army troops. Now, Washington quickly sent more Continental troops under "Mad" Anthony Wayne to reinforce Lafayette.

In August, Cornwallis took his troops into a little Virginia village called Yorktown, located on Chesapeake Bay. Yorktown is on a little piece of land surrounded on three sides by water, with only a narrow strip connecting it to the rest of Virginia. At Yorktown, Cornwallis could receive supplies and reinforcements by sea as well as land.

Clinton Outfoxed, Cornwallis in Trouble

On July 6, Rochambeau and the French Army arrived at Dobbs Ferry, New York, joining forces with Washington and the Continental Army. The two commanders began to talk about the possibility of making an attack on New York City. But on August 14, Rochambeau received a message from the French Admiral de Grasse, indicating that he was sailing to Chesapeake Bay with a powerful fleet of twenty-nine warships. Washington and Rochambeau instantly realized what this meant. If a French fleet was in the bay behind Yorktown, and an American army held the land in front of Yorktown, Cornwallis would not be able to get supplies or reinforcements by land or sea. This would be a terrible problem for him.

All plans for an attack on New York City were cast aside. Washington immediately sent an order to Lafayette to move his army in front of Yorktown and keep Cornwallis there. Then, he and Rochambeau quickly began preparations to march their forces to Yorktown.

This would have to be a fast, secret move. If Clinton found out about it, he might be able to get reinforcements to Cornwallis before the French fleet arrived. However, Washington now showed once again what a clever general he was. He did everything he could to make it look as if he and Rochambeau were preparing to attack New York City. He had his spies in New York state spread rumors about a coming attack on New York City. He wrote fake letters to some of his generals, discussing plans for such an attack—and arranged to have the letters be captured by the British. On August 21, he and Rochambeau started their armies apparently marching toward New York City.

Clinton hurriedly began strengthening fortifications against the attack he expected. But on August 28, the French and Americans suddenly turned south, and by September 2 they were in Philadelphia. Clinton was stunned to realize they were obviously heading for Virginia. He had been tricked out of the chance to send troops to Yorktown, and now it was too late to help Cornwallis.

The Siege of Yorktown

Washington rode ahead of the armies to the place where the men would begin moving down Chesapeake Bay in boats. Rochambeau followed him by boat, and found Washington awaiting him. Washington was usually a very calm, dignified, and serious person, and Rochambeau was astounded to see him jumping about and waving his hat. When the French general stepped onto the dock, Washington actually seized him in a bear hug and whirled him about![7] The reason for Washington's joy was that he had received word the French fleet had arrived in Chesapeake Bay and more than twenty-five hundred French soldiers had landed to join Lafayette's force at the town of Williamsburg.

When Washington and Rochambeau reached Williamsburg with their allied armies, there would be sixteen thousand men in front of Cornwallis, and a French fleet behind him. He would be hopelessly trapped! That afternoon, as the two generals rode southward, a battle began in Chesapeake Bay. A British fleet of nineteen ships commanded by Admiral

Thomas Graves desperately attacked the twenty-nine French ships. Four British ships were severely damaged. The British withdrew from the bay and several days later, sailed for New York. Cornwallis was doomed!

On September 6, the American and French armies began their move into Virginia. Washington was able to visit his home and see his wife for the first time in more than two years. By September 15, all of the American and French forces were assembled at Williamsburg, and the siege of Yorktown began. Cornwallis knew he was in serious trouble. In a letter to Clinton, he said ". . . one cannot hope to make a very long resistance."[8]

Surrender, Peace, a Free New Nation

American and French troops began digging long trenches toward the town so that cannons could be moved as close as possible. After several days, the cannons were in place and Washington himself fired the first shot into Yorktown.[9] From then on, day after day, eighteen- and twenty-four-pound iron balls were crashing into the town's streets and houses, steadily causing casualties. British attempts to capture or damage some of the guns were unsuccessful. So was a British attempt to escape across the river.

Eventually, Cornwallis and his top officers held a council of war and decided the British army in Yorktown could not defeat the siege. It was unable to receive supplies by land or sea, unable to fight its way

It was said that Washington himself fired the first cannon shot of the Siege of Yorktown.

through a force that greatly outnumbered it, and was losing men daily. Its position was hopeless.

At mid-morning on October 16, American soldiers around Yorktown became aware that a small figure had suddenly appeared on one of the British earthworks. It was a British Army drummer boy. He began pounding out what was known as the "parley" beat. This was a repetitive rhythm used by all armies to indicate a wish to have a brief peaceful meeting in order to talk. Moments later, a red-coated officer joined the drummer boy, waving a white handkerchief. This, too, was a signal recognized by all armies as a request for a meeting. Clearly, Cornwallis wanted to talk about terms of surrender. This was the beginning of the end.

Three days later, Cornwallis's soldiers marched out of Yorktown. They piled up their weapons, and were marched off to prison camps. There were still British troops in New York and Charleston, but British commanders were not willing to fight any more battles. In Britain there was no longer any support for continuing the war.

On April 1, 1782, Washington moved most of the army into a camp at the town of Newburgh. He wanted to keep an eye on the British in New York City until they left.

George Washington and his officers (left) receive the surrender of the British army under Charles Cornwallis. This virtually ended the war.

The End of the Continental Army

There was no more fighting, but things were not going well in the new nation. Congress had no money and the soldiers of the Continental Army had not been paid for a long time. By March of 1783, they were on the verge of mutiny. Washington managed to calm them down, and in May most of them began leaving for home.

On September 3, 1783, the final treaties were signed between Great Britain and the United States. The war officially ended. On December 23, Washington went to Congress and officially resigned as commander-in-chief of the Continental Army.

The Continental Army no longer existed. Nothing was left of it. The United States had no army at all for the next nine years. When a new army was formed in 1792, it did not resemble the Continental Army in any way. It had a different uniform, different equipment, and was organized differently. This new army was called The Legion.

George Washington's Continental Army—the United States' first army—kept the American Revolution alive for six-and-a-half years, from Lexington and Concord to the British surrender at Yorktown. Despite battle casualties, short enlistments, desertions, mutinies, starvation, sickness, and the many miseries of Valley Forge and Morristown, there always seemed to be enough men to fight the battles that had to be fought to keep the revolution going. The Continental Army won the vital battles of

EVERY AMERICAN OFFICER AND SOLDIER MUST NOW CONSOLE HIMSELF FOR ANY UNPLEASANT CIRCUMSTANCES WHICH MAY HAVE OCCURRED BY A RECOLLECTION OF THE UNCOMMON SCENES IN WHICH HE HAS BEEN CALLED TO ACT NO INGLORIOUS PART, AND THE ASTONISHING EVENTS OF WHICH HE HAS BEEN A WITNESS, EVENTS WHICH HAVE SELDOM IF EVER BEFORE TAKEN PLACE ON THE STAGE OF HUMAN ACTION, NOR CAN THEY PROBABLY EVER HAPPEN AGAIN. FOR WHO HAS BEFORE SEEN A DISCIPLINED ARMY FORM'D AT ONCE FROM SUCH RAW MATERIALS? WHO, THAT WAS NOT A WITNESS, COULD IMAGINE THAT THE MOST VIOLENT LOCAL PREJUDICES WOULD CEASE SO SOON, AND THAT MEN WHO CAME FROM THE DIFFERENT PARTS OF THE CONTINENT, STRONGLY DISPOSED [INCLINED], BY THE HABITS OF EDUCATION, TO DESPISE AND QUARREL WITH EACH OTHER, WOULD INSTANTLY BECOME BUT ONE PATRIOTIC BAND OF BROTHERS, OR WHO, THAT WAS NOT ON THE SPOT, CAN TRACE THE STEPS BY WHICH SUCH A WONDERFUL REVOLUTION HAS BEEN EFFECTED, AND SUCH A GLORIOUS PERIOD PUT TO ALL OUR WARLIKE TOILS?[10]

In his farewell orders to the Continental Army, General Washington outlines the great accomplishments that the revolutionary forces have achieved.

Trenton, Princeton, and Monmouth. Soldiers of the Continental Army, parceled out by Washington, provided the core for little armies of state militia that won the victories in New York that were the war's turning point. They fought in battles in the South that held the states together.

Under George Washington's leadership, with the help of such men as von Steuben, Lafayette, Greene, Morgan, and Knox, the Continental Army grew beyond its origin as a ragtag mob of brave but inexperienced farmers and workingmen. It became a real army of disciplined, battlewise soldiers who could hold their own against any opponent. This was the army that brought the United States its freedom.

★ TIMELINE ★

1775—*April 19*: British troops and Massachusetts minutemen fight at Lexington and Concord.

June 15: George Washington is appointed commander-in-chief of all American forces.

June 17: The British win the Battle of Bunker Hill, but take enormous casualties.

July 3: Washington officially takes command of the Continental Army at Boston; At once, he begins reorganizing the Army and tightening discipline.

August 28: An American force of twelve hundred men commanded by Brigadier General Richard Montgomery begins the invasion of Canada.

September 12: Washington sends 1,050 Continental Army troops to Canada under the command of Benedict Arnold.

1776—*January 24*: Colonel Henry Knox begins bringing fifty-five cannons, taken from Fort Ticonderoga, to the Continental Army near Boston; Washington can now threaten to attack the city.

March 27: The British evacuate Boston.

April 13: Washington starts the army marching to New York.

June 24: The American attempt to conquer Canada ends in complete failure.

July 4: Congress adopts the final draft of the Declaration of Independence.

August 22: Fifteen thousand British and Hessian troops attack Washington's forces on Long Island, New York.

August 29: Washington evacuates his troops into New York City, saving his army.

September 15: The British attack New York City; Washington withdraws to nearby Harlem Heights.

September 16: Washington wins a small victory at Harlem Heights.

December 26: Washington leads an attack against a Hessian brigade in Trenton, New Jersey, and wins a stunning victory.

1777—*January 3*: With another surprise attack, Washington wins another victory at Princeton, New Jersey.

July 1: A British army led by General Burgoyne invades New York from Canada.

July 23: British General Howe leaves New York with eighteen thousand men in ships, sailing to an unknown destination.

August 16: Part of Burgoyne's army is wiped out by an American militia force.

August 23: Washington marches his army to Philadelphia in case Howe attacks there.

September 11: Washington is beaten by Howe at Brandywine Creek, Pennsylvania.

October 4: Washington attacks the British at Germantown, but has to withdraw.

October 7: The American army in New York nearly destroys Burgoyne's army.

October 17: Burgoyne surrenders at Saratoga, New York.

December 19: The Continental Army goes into winter quarters at Valley Forge.

1778—*February 6*: France signs a treaty of alliance with the United States.

February 23: Baron Von Steuben arrives at Valley Forge to begin his training program.

June 16: British forces, now commanded by General Clinton, leave Philadelphia.

June 28: Washington engages Clinton at Monmouth Court House, in New Jersey. Clinton is forced to withdraw.

July 6: Clinton takes his army to New York City; Washington and his army follow.

December 29: A British force captures the seaport of Savannah, in Georgia.

1779—*October 9*: An attack against Savannah by American and French forces fails.

1780—*February 1*: Eighty-five hundred British troops arrive at Savannah and march to Charleston.

May 12: General Benjamin Lincoln surrenders Charleston to the British.

July 10: A fleet of French ships arrives at Newport, Rhode Island, bringing a French army of six thousand troops to America.

August 16: An American force is badly defeated at Camden, South Carolina.

September 25: Washington learns Benedict Arnold has gone over to the British.

October 7: General Nathanael Greene takes command of the Continental Army in the South.

1781—*January 17*: Part of Greene's army wins a striking victory at the Battle of Cowpens in South Carolina.

August 5: British General Cornwallis takes his army into Yorktown, Virginia.

August 21: Washington and Rochambeau start their armies marching to Yorktown.

September 28: The Siege of Yorktown begins.

October 19: Cornwallis surrenders; With the help of the French, the Continental Army has effectively won the war.

1782—*April 1*: Washington gathers most of the Army together in camp at Newburgh, New York.

1783—*May 26*: The men of the Continental Army are ordered to return home.

December 23: Washington goes to Congress and resigns as commander-in-chief; The Continental Army no longer exists.

★ CHAPTER NOTES ★

Chapter 1. An April Morning in 1775

1. Thomas Fleming, *Liberty! The American Revolution* (New York: Viking Penguin, 1997), p. 109.

2. Richard M. Ketchum, *Saratoga: Turning Point of America's Revolutionary War* (New York: Henry Holt and Company, 1997), p. 67.

3. Fleming, p. 88.

4. Benson Bobrick, *Angel in the Whirlwind: the Triumph of the American Revolution* (New York: Simon & Schuster, 1997), p. 116.

5. "Journals of the Continental Congress—Thursday, May, 11, 1775," *Library of Congress—American Memory, A Century of Lawmaking for a New Nation: U.S. Congressional Documents and Debates, 1774–1875*, May 11, 1775 < http://memory.loc.gov/cgi-bin/query/r?ammem/hlaw:@field(DOCID+@lit(jc0026)):> (May 30, 2003).

6. Fleming, p. 116.

7. Henry Carrington, *Battles of the American Revolution* (New York: Promontory Press, 1974), p. 11.

8. Ibid.

Chapter 2. Boston Besieged

1. Richard M. Ketchum, *Decisive Day: The Battle for Bunker Hill* (New York: Anchor Books, Doubleday, 1974), p. 4.

2. "Journals of the Continental Congress—Thursday, May, 18, 1775," *Library of Congress—American Memory, A Century of Lawmaking for a New Nation: U.S. Congressional Documents and Debates, 1774–1875*, May 18, 1775 < http://memory.loc.gov/cgi-bin/query/r?ammem/hlaw:@field(DOCID+@lit(jc00212)):> (June 2, 2003).

3. Thomas Fleming, *Now We Are Enemies: The Story of Bunker Hill* (New York: St. Martin's Press, 1960), p. 128.

4. Thomas Fleming, *Liberty! The American Revolution* (New York: Viking Penguin, 1997), p. 133.

Chapter 3. The Battle of Bunker Hill

1. "Journals of the Continental Congress—Thursday, June 14, 1775," *Library of Congress—American Memory, A Century of Lawmaking for a New Nation: U.S. Congressional Documents and Debates, 1774–1875*, June 14, 1775 < http://memory.loc.gov/cgi-bin/query/r?ammem/ hlaw:@field(DOCID+@lit(jc0235)):> (May 30, 2003).

2. Craig L. Symonds, *A Battlefield Atlas of the American Revolution* (Mt. Pleasant: S.C.: The Nautical and Aviation Publishing Company of America, Inc., 1986), p. 1.

3. William M. Marsh, "Bunker Hill," *Command: Military History, Strategy, and Analysis*, January/February 1995, Issue 38, p. 20.

4. L. Edward Purcell and David F. Burg, ed., *The World Almanac of the American Revolution* (New York: World Almanac, 1992), p. 47.

5. Richard M. Ketchum, *Decisive Day: The Battle for Bunker Hill* (New York: Anchor Books, Doubleday, 1974), p. 162.

6. Thomas Fleming, *Now We Are Enemies: The Story of Bunker Hill* (New York: St. Martin's Press, 1960), p. 270.

7. Fleming, *Liberty: The American Revolution* (New York: Viking Penguin, 1997), p. 141.

8. Fleming, *Now We Are Enemies: The Story of Bunker Hill*, p. 321.

Chapter 4. General Washington Takes Command

1. Craig L. Symonds, *A Battlefield Atlas of the American Revolution* (Mt. Pleasant: S.C.: The Nautical and Aviation Publishing Company of America, 1986), p. 19.

2. Thomas Fleming, *Now We Are Enemies: The Story of Bunker Hill* (New York: St. Martin's Press, 1960), p. 332.

3. L. Edward Purcell and David F. Burg, ed., *The World Almanac of the American Revolution* (New York: World Almanac, 1992), p. 52.

4. George Washington, "George Washington, July 3, 1775, General Orders," *Library of Congress—American Memory, The George Washington Papers at the Library of Congress, 1741–1799*, July 3, 1775 <http://memory.loc.gov/cgi-bin/query/r?ammem/mgw:@field(DOCID+@lit(gw030218)):> (May 30, 2003).

5. Thomas Fleming, *Liberty! The American Revolution* (New York: Viking Penguin, 1997), p. 147.

Chapter 5. Setbacks in New York

1. Thomas Fleming, *Liberty! The American Revolution* (New York: Viking Penguin, 1997), p. 186.

2. Robert H. Harrison, "George Washington to Continental Congress, August 27, 1776," *Library of Congress—American Memory, The George Washington Papers at the Library of Congress, 1741–1799*, August 27, 1776 <http://memory.loc.gov/cgi-bin/query/r?ammem/mgw:@field(DOCID+@lit(gw050426)):> (May 30, 2003).

3. Milton Lomask, *The First American Revolution* (New York: Farrar, Straus and Giroux, 1974), p. 168.

4. Henry Carrington, *Battles of the American Revolution, 1775–1781* (New York: Promontory Press, 1974), pp. 240–241.

Chapter 6. Some Victories and a Serious Defeat

1. Richard M. Ketchum, *The Winter Soldiers* (New York: Doubleday & Company, Inc., 1973), p. 295.

2. Henry B. Carrington, *Battles of the American Revolution, 1775–1781* (New York, Promontory Press, 1887), p. 274.

3. George Washington, "George Washington to Alexander McDougall, December 28, 1776," *Library of Congress—American Memory, The George Washington Papers at the Library of Congress, 1741–1799*, December 28, 1776 < http://memory.loc.gov/cgi-bin/query/r?ammem/ mgw:@field(DOCID+@lit(gw060341)):> (May 30, 2003).

4. Ketchum, p. 344.

5. Fairfax Downey, *Sound of the Guns* (New York: David McKay Company, Inc., 1955), p. 49.

6. Craig L. Symonds, *A Battlefield Atlas of the American Revolution* (Mt. Pleasant: S.C.: The Nautical and Aviation Publishing Company of America, Inc., 1986), p. 45.

7. Ibid.

8. Milton Lomask, *The First American Revolution* (New York: Farrar, Straus and Giroux, 1974), p. 194.

Chapter 7. Rebuilding an Army

1. Craig L. Symonds, *A Battlefield Atlas of the American Revolution* (Mt. Pleasant: S.C.: The Nautical and Aviation Publishing Company of America, Inc., 1986), p. 55.

2. George Washington, "George Washington to Patrick Henry, February 19, 1778," *Library of Congress—American Memory, The George Washington Papers at the Library of Congress, 1741–1799*, February 19, 1778 < http://memory.loc.gov/cgi-bin/query/r?ammem/ mgw:@field(DOCID+@lit(gw100450)):> (May 30, 2003).

3. Benson Bobrick, *Angel in the Whirlwind: the Triumph of the American Revolution* (New York: Simon & Schuster, 1997), p. 345.

4. Ibid.

5. David R. Wade, "Washington Saves the Day at Monmouth," *Military History* (June, 1998), p. 53.

Chapter 8. Victory in Virginia

1. Craig L. Symonds, *A Battlefield Atlas of the American Revolution* (Mt. Pleasant: S.C.: The Nautical and Aviation Publishing Company of America, Inc., 1986), p. 75.

2. Page Smith, *A New Age Now Begins: A People's History of the American Revolution*, Volume Two (New York: McGraw-Hill Book Company, 1976), pp. 1306–1307.

3. Edward Purcell and David F. Burg, ed., *The World Almanac of the American Revolution* (New York: World Almanac, 1992), p. 225.

4. Thomas Fleming, *Liberty! The American Revolution* (New York: Viking Penguin, 1997), p. 311.

5. Ibid., p. 314.

6. Ibid., p. 316.

7. Symonds, p. 101.

8. Henry B. Carrington, *Battles of the American Revolution, 1775–1781* (New York: Promontory Press, 1887), p. 638.

9. Purcell and Burg, p. 289.

10. George Washington, "George Washington to Continental Army, November 2, 1783, Farewell Orders," *Library of Congress—American Memory, The George Washington Papers at the Library of Congress, 1741–1799,* November 2, 1783 <http://memory.loc.gov/cgi-bin/query/r?ammem/mgw:@field(DOCID+@lit(gw270250)):> (May 30, 2003).

★ GLOSSARY ★

bayonet—The blade at the end of a musket or rifle.

breastwork—A wall, sometimes extending out from a fort, that is built to protect soldiers.

breeches—Pants with cuffs that fit tightly around the knee.

cartridge—A paper container holding gunpowder and a lead ball for use in a musket.

casualties—Soldiers lost during war; usually refers to the dead, wounded, or captured.

cavalry—Soldiers on horses.

company—A military unit. A number of companies make up a regiment. A company in the Continental Army had about ninety men, and eight companies typically made up a regiment.

division—A large military unit, made up of a number of regiments. The Continental Army had three divisions.

drill (v.)—To train soldiers by making them practice the movements they will need to make in battle.

flank—The left or right side of a line of soldiers.

flintlock—A small hammer-like device on a musket that was used to ignite the gunpowder, causing a small explosion that propelled a lead ball out of the musket's barrel.

ford—A shallow part of a river where people can wade across.

grenadier—A member of a special force of the British Army.

Hessian—A German soldier, usually from the region of Hesse-Kassel, who fought for the British.

light infantry—British soldiers trained to move and fight fast. The bayonet charge was the most common maneuver of these soldiers.

marksman—A soldier who could hit the enemy from far away. Marksmen often had rifling on the inside of their musket barrels.

militia—Small bands of volunteer, part-time soldiers who were organized to protect the colonies.

minutemen—Massachusetts militia who were said to be ready to fight at a minute's notice.

musket—The typical gun used by soldiers in the late eighteenth-century. It had to be reloaded after each shot fired.

peninsula—A piece of land surrounded by water on all but one side. Florida is a good example of a peninsula.

ramrod—The rod used to pack the cartridge paper, gunpowder, and lead ball tightly in a musket's barrel.

redcoat—A British soldier.

regiment—A military unit, made up of several companies. A division consisted of a number of regiments. Continental Army regiments usually each consisted of 728 soldiers and officers. Although a British regiment was supposed to have 477 troops, those in the colonies had only between 300 and 400.

rifling—Spiral grooves inside the barrels of some muskets that made the guns more accurate.

siege—A military tactic that consists of a group of soldiers surrounding a city that is occupied by the enemy. Sieges cut off supplies and food from getting into the city. Eighteenth-century soldiers laying siege fired cannons into the enemy-occupied city to cause casualties.

spur (v.)—To make a horse gallop faster by hitting it with a pointed piece of metal, called a spur, attached to one's riding boots.

Tory—An American colonist loyal to Britain.

tricorn—A three-cornered hat that was worn by many American militiamen.

volley—The firing of a number of muskets at the same time.

Whig—An American colonist who wanted to be free from Britain's rule.

★ FURTHER READING ★

Aaseng, Nathan. *Strategic Battles*. Farmington Hills, Mich.: Gale Group, 2002.

Bullock, Steven C. *The American Revolution: A History in Documents*. New York, Oxford University Press, 2003.

Cooper, Paul. *Going to War in the 18th Century*. Danbury, Conn.: Children's Press, 2001.

Harmon, Dan. *Fighting Units of the American War of Independence*. Philadelphia: Chelsea House Publishers, 1999.

January, Brendan. *George Washington*. Danbury, Conn.: Scholastic Library Publishing, 2003.

King, David C. *Lexington and Concord*. New York: Twenty-First Century Books, 1997

———. *Saratoga*. New York: Twenty-First Century Books, 1998.

Nash, Gary. *Landmarks of the American Revolution*. New York: Oxford University Press, 2003.

Parker, Lewis K. *The Battle of Monmouth*. Farmington Hills, Mich.: Gale Group, 2002.

———. *The Battle of Trenton*. Farmington Hills, Mich.: Gale Group, 2002.

Weber, Michael. *Yorktown*. New York: Twenty-First Century Books, 1997.

★ INTERNET ADDRESSES ★

McGranahan, Ronald W. "The Continental Army." *The American Revolution Home Page*. © 1998–2002. <http://www.americanrevwar.homestead.com/files/CONTAR.HTM>.

The National Park Service. "Dig It: Experience an Archeological Dig at Valley Forge." April 7, 2003. <http://www.cr.nps.gov/logcabin/html/dig_it.html>.

PBS Online and Twin Cities Public Television. "The Continental Army." *Liberty! Chronicle of the Revolution*. © 1997. <http://www.pbs.org/ktca/liberty/chronicle/continental.army.html>.

★ INDEX ★

20.95
6/04